Do You Think What You Think You Think?

The Ultimate Philosophical Handbook

JULIAN BAGGINI AND JEREMY STANGROOM

A PLUME BOOK

PLUME
Published by Penguin Group
Penguin Group (USA) Inc., 375 Hudson Street, New York, New York 10014, U.S.A. •
Penguin Group (Canada), 90 Eglinton Avenue East, Suite 700, Toronto, Ontario,
Canada M4P 2Y3 (a division of Pearson Penguin Canada Inc.) • Penguin Books Ltd., 80
Strand, London WC2R 0RL, England • Penguin Ireland, 25 St. Stephen's Green, Dublin 2,
Ireland (a division of Penguin Books Ltd.) • Penguin Group (Australia), 250 Camberwell
Road, Camberwell, Victoria 3124, Australia (a division of Pearson Australia Group Pty.
Ltd.) • Penguin Books India Pvt. Ltd., 11 Community Centre, Panchsheel Park, New
Delhi – 110 017, India • Penguin Group (NZ), 67 Apollo Drive, Rosedale, North Shore
0745, Auckland, New Zealand (a division of Pearson New Zealand Ltd.) • Penguin Books
(South Africa) (Pty.) Ltd., 24 Sturdee Avenue, Rosebank, Johannesburg 2196,
South Africa

Penguin Books Ltd., Registered Offices: 80 Strand, London WC2R 0RL, England

Published by Plume, a member of Penguin Group (USA) Inc. Originally published in
Great Britain by Granta Publications.

First American Printing, September 2007
10 9 8 7 6 5 4 3 2 1

 REGISTERED TRADEMARK—MARCA REGISTRADA

LIBRARY OF CONGRESS CATALOGING-IN-PUBLICATION DATA
Baggini, Julian.
   Do you think what you think you think? : the ultimate philosophical handbook /
Julian Baggini and Jeremy Stangroom.
      p. cm.
   ISBN 978-0-452-28865-2 (trade pbk.)
      1. Philosophy—Miscellanea.   I. Stangroom, Jeremy.   II. Title.
      BD31. B28   2007
      100—dc22

                                                            2007003089

Printed in the United States of America

Contents

Acknowledgments

Thanks to George Miller and Gail Lynch for supporting the idea of this book; TPM Online (www.philosophersnet.com) mailing list members for beta testing many of the activities in their previous, online form; Ophelia Benson; and Sajidah Ahmad, Lesley Levene, Daphne Trotter, Joanna Macnamara for their thorough checking. Any mistakes that remain are entirely our responsibility.

"The Philosophical Health Check" is based on an original idea by Marilyn Mason.

"So You Think You're Logical?" is inspired by original work by Peter Wason, Leda Cosmides and John Tooby.

"The Do-It-Yourself Deity" is based on an original idea by Jeremy Hayward and Gerald Jones, whose numerous books by Hodder Murray are strongly recommended, especially for teachers looking to introduce philosophical activities to the classroom.

"Taboo" is inspired largely by the work of Jonathan Haidt, Silvia Helena Koller and Maria G. Dias.

David Cooper's *Aesthetics: The Classic Readings* (Blackwell) provided many of the sources for our summary of the major philosophical theories of art in "Shakespeare vs. Britney Spears" and is highly recommended for those wishing to find out more about them.

This book emerged out of our work with *The Philosophers' Magazine*, which has only survived with the support of numerous generous contributors and individuals such as Ophelia Benson, Denis Collins, Jonathan Derbyshire, Susan Dwyer, Simon Eassom, Peter Fosl, Wendy Grossman, Mathew Iredale, Michael LaBossiere, Jeff Mason, Scott McLemee, Christopher Norris and Christian Perring; as well, of course, as our readers.

Introduction

Know thyself.

Inscription at the Temple of Apollo in Delphi

There's no doubting that Descartes was a pretty clever guy. But whether it was his fault or that of his acolytes, a lot of hopeless misconceptions about human nature can be traced back to him. Of all these, perhaps the greatest is the "incorrigibility of the mental": the belief that we cannot be mistaken about the contents of our own minds. I think I feel pain, so I do feel pain, and there's no way I can be mistaken about that. If I can see an elephant, then I may be hallucinating and there is no elephant there, but nonetheless, it has to be true that I am having the experience of seeing an elephant. If your coat looks yellow to me, the fact that it is really green doesn't change the fact that it looks yellow to me.

But the simple truth is that we can be horribly, tragically, painfully wrong about what is in our heads. Just think of the kinds of things people say all the time. I thought I was in love but really it was just lust. I thought I had indigestion but actually I was pregnant. I thought I believed in socialism but when I saw my tax bill I realized that I didn't. I thought I didn't want my children to be different but actually I wanted them to change so I could be closer to them. I thought I enjoyed working long hours but really I was kidding myself and I was just avoiding issues in my personal life. I thought I was

1

being honest but actually I was holding back crucial information and deceiving him.

What we "really" think is an incredibly difficult area. The purpose of this book is to provide you with some entertaining ways of thinking about what and how you think, and to reveal some surprising things about both. By the end of it, we think you may well find yourself thinking that what you think you think is no longer what you thought you thought. And like that last sentence, that may be disconcerting, a little confusing, but actually quite good fun.

Visit this book's Web site at www.doyouthinkwhatyouthink.com.

How to use this book

1 Grab a pen or a pencil. A pencil is good for *you*, because it means you can always erase your answers and use the book again yourself, or pass it on to others. (A pen is good for *us* because you can't, so if you do enjoy it, you'll have to buy more copies.)

2 Don't be defensive. Be prepared to be wrong and also to argue back if you disagree with us. But not in e-mails, phone calls or heckles in public places, please.

3 Go through each activity slowly and carefully. There is nothing so complicated that a bright child couldn't follow it, but if you rush or skip steps, you'll end up more confused than an atheist finding himself at the pearly gates with Margaret Thatcher standing guard only letting in Orthodox Greeks.

4 Don't worry about whether this book is serious or not. To do so is to worry about a bogus distinction. As Wittgenstein said, "A serious and good philosophical work could be written consisting entirely of jokes." Or, in this case, games.

1

The Philosophical Health Check

I have opinions of my own—strong opinions—but I don't always agree with them.

George W. Bush

Clint Eastwood once memorably said, "Opinions are like assholes—everybody has one." With our own beliefs, however, we do not wish our viewpoints to resemble any part or function of rectums in any other way. Other people's views may be foolish, ill-considered, naive or wicked, but our own are considered, intelligent and well worth listening to.

Well, perhaps. The purpose of the Philosophical Health Check, however, is not to tell you which of your opinions are true and which are false. What it will do is reveal something about how well you've thought them through. To push Eastwood's metaphor further than it is perhaps decent to do, we'll find out if your opinions are like two well-toned buttocks or a flabby backside.

Take the check

To take the Philosophical Health Check, go through the statements below, deciding for each one whether you agree or disagree. At this stage it is important that you simply mark your answers as you go along or jot them onto a piece of paper. Do not look at the marking grid or analysis that follows until you have answered the questions.

We know that you will not always agree or disagree 100%, but almost always you will tend more toward one answer than the other. If you're not sure, select the response that is closest to your opinion. If you really have no opinion at all, it's time you got one!

The Philosophical Health Check does not judge whether your responses are right or wrong, so answer as honestly as you can. Every statement is carefully worded, so pay attention to what each one actually says.

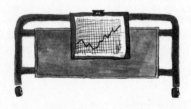

	Agree	Disagree
1 There are no objective moral standards; moral judgments are merely an expression of the values of particular cultures.		
2 So long as they do not harm others, individuals should be free to pursue their own ends.		
3 People should not travel by car if they can walk, cycle or take a train instead.		
4 It is always wrong to take another person's life.		
5 The right to life is so fundamental that financial considerations are irrelevant in any effort to save lives.		
6 Voluntary euthanasia should remain illegal.		
7 Homosexuality is wrong because it is unnatural.		
8 It is quite reasonable to believe in the existence of a thing without even the possibility of evidence for its existence.		
9 The possession of drugs for personal use should be decriminalized.		
10 There exists an all-powerful, loving and good God.		

		Agree	Disagree
11	The Second World War was a just war.		
12	Having made a choice, it is always possible that one might have chosen otherwise.		
13	It is not always right to judge individuals solely on their merits.		
14	Judgments about works of art are purely matters of taste.		
15	On bodily death, a person continues to exist in a nonphysical form.		
16	The government should not permit the sale of health treatments that have not been tested for efficacy and safety.		
17	There are no objective truths about matters of fact; "truth" is always relative to particular cultures and individuals.		
18	Atheism is a faith just like any other, because it is not possible to prove the nonexistence of God.		
19	Proper sanitation and medicines are generally good for a society.		
20	In certain circumstances, it might be desirable to discriminate positively in favor of a person as recompense for harms done to him/her in the past.		

		Agree	Disagree
21	Alternative and complementary medicines are as valuable as mainstream medicine.		
22	Severe brain damage can rob a person of all consciousness and selfhood.		
23	To allow an innocent child to suffer needlessly when one could easily prevent it is morally reprehensible.		
24	The environment should not be damaged unnecessarily in the pursuit of human ends.		
25	Michelangelo is one of history's finest artists.		
26	Individuals have sole rights over their own bodies.		
27	Acts of genocide stand as a testament to man's ability to do great evil.		
28	The Holocaust is a historical reality that took place more or less as the history books report.		
29	Governments should be allowed to increase taxes sharply to save lives in the developing world.		
30	The future is fixed; how one's life unfolds is a matter of destiny.		

How to score

Under each heading T1–T15, put a tick in all of the boxes that match your answers (T is for Tension, Q is for Question).

T1	T2	T3	T4	T5
Q1 Agree	Q5 Agree	Q10 Agree	Q17 Agree	Q24 Agree
Q27 Agree	Q29 Disagree	Q23 Agree	Q28 Agree	Q3 Disagree

T6	T7	T8	T9	T10
Q2 Agree	Q26 Agree	Q4 Agree	Q12 Agree	Q19 Agree
Q9 Disagree	Q6 Agree	Q11 Agree	Q30 Agree	Q7 Agree

T11	T12	T13	T14	T15
Q20 Agree	Q22 Agree	Q8 Disagree	Q14 Agree	Q16 Agree
Q13 Disagree	Q15 Agree	Q18 Agree	Q25 Agree	Q21 Agree

Every time you tick two boxes in the same column, T1–T15, we have identified one tension in your belief system. We'll explain what that means later, but because you probably want to know your score first, here's what we think it implies.

No tensions   Your opinions on the issues we asked you about are totally consistent.

1 & 2 tensions   You seem to be an admirably consistent thinker, if not entirely so.

3–5 tensions   Like most people, your opinions probably don't hang together as well as they might.

6+ tensions   You're either an incredibly subtle thinker or a mass of contradictions!

General analysis

The Philosophical Health Check is designed to identify tensions or contradictions between various beliefs that you have. It does not aim to identify which of your beliefs are true or false, but potential incompatibilities in the set of beliefs you hold.

Each tension we have identified indicates *either* that (1) there is a contradiction between the two beliefs *or* (2) some sophisticated reasoning is required to enable both beliefs to be held consistently. In each case, this means that there are reasons, which we will shortly explain, that make holding both beliefs at the same time very difficult, if not impossible.

You can think of the idea of "tension" in terms of an intellectual balancing act. Where there is little or no tension between beliefs, little intellectual effort is required to balance both beliefs. But where there is a lot of tension, one has to "jump off the tightrope" by abandoning one belief, maintain one's balance by intellectual effort and dexterity, or else "fall off the tightrope" by failing to reconcile the tension and continuing to hold contradictory beliefs.

Should you be worried about the tensions we have identified? If you care at all about being consistent, then you should *either* (1) give up one of the two beliefs *or* (2) find some rationally coherent way of reconciling them. If you think you don't care about consistency, perhaps you should.

Note that this test only detects tensions between preselected pairs of beliefs—it does not detect all the possible tensions between all permutations of beliefs. So there may well be additional tensions between beliefs you hold that are not detected by the test. A top score does not indicate perfect consistency through all your beliefs.

The tensions explained

In this section we explain why each of the tensions we have identified among the thirty beliefs is indeed a tension. You might like just to read about the tensions in your own beliefs, but you may also find it interesting to find out about some of the other traps you managed to avoid—perhaps to help you catch your friends in them. We also tell you how many people out of a sample of 80,000 who have taken a version of this test online have each tension in their beliefs.

Tension 1: Is morality relative?

This tension arises when someone agrees that: *There are no objective moral standards; moral judgments are merely an expression of the values of particular cultures* and also that *Acts of genocide stand as a testament to man's ability to do great evil.* Nearly half of our respondents exhibited this tension.

The tension between these two beliefs is that, while one of them claims that morality is just a matter of culture and convention, the other condemns acts of genocide as "evil." But the claim that "genocide is evil" seems to go beyond mere culture and convention. It is just about possible to say that "genocide is evil" merely expresses the values of a particular culture and does not mean that genocide is evil for all cultures and for all times. However, few are really prepared to accept the logical implications of this view and say that, for example, the 1994 massacre of Rwandan Tutsis by the Hutu Interahamwe and Impuzamugambi militia was evil from the point of view of your culture but not evil from the point of view of the Hutus, and there is no sense in which one moral judgment is superior to the other. But if moral judgments really are merely the "expression of the values of a particular culture," then how are the values that reject genocide and torture at all superior to those that do not?

Tension 2: Can you put a price on a human life?

This tension arises when someone agrees that *The right to life is so fundamental that financial considerations are irrelevant in any effort to save lives* but disagrees that *Governments should be allowed to increase taxes sharply to save lives in the developing world.* Around a quarter of the people in our research had this tension.

If the right to life is so fundamental that financial considerations are irrelevant when it comes to making decisions about saving human lives, then that must mean that we should always spend as much money as possible to save lives. If it costs $4 million to save a cancer patient's life, that money should be spent, period. But if this is true, then surely the West should spend as much money as possible saving lives in the developing world. You may already give $100 a month to save lives in the developing world. But if financial considerations are irrelevant when it comes to saving lives, why not $200, or $1,000, or just as much as you can afford? If you do not do so, you are implicitly endorsing the principle that individuals and governments are not obliged to save lives at all financial cost—that one can spend "enough" on saving lives even though spending more, which one could afford to do, would save more lives. This suggests that although financial considerations *are* relevant when it comes to making decisions about saving lives, there is a limit to how much one should spend to save a life.

Tension 3: Is there an all-good, all-powerful God?

This tension arises when someone agrees that *There exists an all-powerful, loving and good God* and also that *To allow an*

14

innocent child to suffer needlessly when one could easily prevent it is morally reprehensible. Around a third of the people in our research had this tension in their beliefs.

These two beliefs together generate what is known as "The Problem of Evil." The problem is simple: If God is all-powerful, loving and good, that means he can do what he wants and will do what is morally right. But surely this means that he would not allow an innocent child to suffer needlessly, as he could easily prevent it. Yet he does. Much infant suffering is the result of human action, but much is also due to natural causes, such as disease, flood or famine. In all cases, God could stop it, yet he does not.

Attempts to explain this apparent contradiction are known as "theodicies" and many have been produced. Most conclude that God allows suffering to help us grow spiritually and/or to allow the greater good of human freedom. Whether these theodicies are adequate is the subject of continuing debate.

Tension 4: Are there any absolute truths?

This tension is between agreeing both that *There are no objective truths about matters of fact; "truth" is always relative to particular cultures and individuals* and also that *The Holocaust is a historical reality that took place more or less as the history books report*. It's a tension more than one third of online respondents exhibited.

If truth is relative then nothing is straightforwardly "true" or "factual." Everything is "true for someone" or "a fact for them." What, then, of the Holocaust? Is it true that millions of Jews, Gypsies, homosexuals and other "enemies" of the Third Reich were systematically executed by the Nazis? If you believe that there are no objective truths, you have to say that there is no straight answer to this question. For some people, the

Holocaust is a fact; for others, it is not. So what can you say to those who deny it is a fact? Are they not as entitled to their view as you are to yours? How can one both assert the reality of the Holocaust and deny that there is a single truth about it? Resolving this intellectual tension is a real challenge, which is why many prefer, on reflection, to conclude there are objective truths after all.

Tension 5: How much must I protect the environment?

This is the most common tension we have uncovered: about half of the people we surveyed were shown to hold this tension, which arises when someone agrees that *The environment should not be damaged unnecessarily in the pursuit of human ends* but disagrees that *People should not travel by car if they can walk, cycle or take a train instead.*

As walking, cycling and taking the train are all less environmentally damaging than driving a car for the same journey, if you choose to drive when you could have used another mode of transport, you are guilty of unnecessarily damaging the environment.

The problem here is the word *unnecessarily*. Very few things are necessary, if by *necessary* it is meant essential to survival. But you might want to argue that much of your use of cars or airplanes is necessary, not for survival, but for a certain quality of life. The danger in this response is that *necessary* simply comes to mean what one judges to be important for oneself. A single plane journey may add more pollutants to the atmosphere than a year's use of a high-emission vehicle. Who is guilty of causing unnecessary environmental harm here?

Tension 6: Can we please ourselves?

This tension is a product of agreeing that *So long as they do not harm others, individuals should be free to pursue their own ends* but disagreeing that *The possession of drugs for personal use should be decriminalized*. Although this tension is less common than some others, nearly three respondents in ten had it.

In order not to be in contradiction here, you must be able to make a convincing case that the personal use of drugs harms people other than the drug user. More than this—you must also show that prohibited drug use harms others more than legal activities such as smoking, drinking and driving cars, unless you want to argue that these should also be made criminal offenses. As alcohol, tobacco and car accidents are among the leading killers in Western society, this case may be hard to make. You also have to make the case for each drug you think should not be decriminalized. The set of drugs that are currently illegal is not a natural one, so there is no reason to treat all currently illegal drugs the same.

Tension 7: Can I make choices about my own body?

This tension is caused by agreeing that *Individuals have sole rights over their own bodies* and also that *Voluntary euthanasia should remain illegal*. Only around one in eight of our respondents had this tension.

Why, if individuals have sole rights over their own bodies, should voluntary euthanasia be illegal? This appears to be a straight contradiction. Ways around this might include adding a condition to the first principle, to the effect that "except when it comes to decisions of life and death." But what would justify this added condition? It might be argued that euthanasia is different because it requires third-party assistance. Yet

17

normally we do not think that the right a person has over their body is forfeited if a third party is involved. If I want a tattoo, I need third-party assistance. But, assuming I can find a willing tattooist, this doesn't mean I don't have sole right to decide whether or not I am tattooed.

Tension 8: Is killing always wrong?

This tension arises when someone agrees that *It is always wrong to take another person's life* and also that *The Second World War was a just war*. Only around one in nine of our subjects had this tension in their beliefs.

It is clear here that someone who has this tension must either give up the idea of a just war or get rid of the "always" in the principle "It is always wrong to take another person's life." It is actually very difficult to add to this principle a clause that starts "except," so that it both allows the kind of killing many feel is justified, yet keeps out the kind of killing that is felt to be unjustified. For example, "except in self-defense" might seem reasonable, but this would mean an army could fight only when attacked and could never risk civilian casualties. One also has to be careful that the "except" clause is thought-out and justifiable, and not merely an ad hoc device to justify what we feel is right and keep out what we don't like. There must be some better foundation to it than that for the principle to have teeth.

Tension 9: Is the future fixed?

Around one in eight people surveyed agreed that *Having made a choice, it is always possible that one might have chosen otherwise* and also that *The future is fixed; how one's life unfolds is a matter of destiny*, thus revealing a tension in their beliefs.

Most people think that humans have free will. Yet many of the same people believe in fate or destiny. How can both beliefs be true? If "what will be, will be" no matter what we do, then how can we have freedom? For example, imagine I am in a shop, deciding whether to buy one of two coats. If one believes in fate or destiny, then it must be true that it is inevitable which coat I buy. In which case, when I stand before them, choosing, it must be an illusion that I have a genuine choice, as fate has decreed that there is, in fact, only one choice I can make. I seem to be making up my own mind, but forces beyond my control have already determined which way I choose. This makes it untrue that "Having made a choice, it is always possible that one might have chosen otherwise." So reconciling belief in destiny and free will is a tricky task.

Tension 10: Is the unnatural wrong?

There is indeed a tension between holding that *Proper sanitation and medicines are generally good for a society* and also that *Homosexuality is wrong because it is unnatural*, even though any connection at all between the two statements may not be obvious. One in eight of our respondents had this tension.

Most people believe that sanitation and medicine are good. But aren't they unnatural? What is natural about sophisticated modern sewage systems and the domestic supply of clean water? What is natural about chemotherapy or other advanced medical treatments? So the first problem here is that it is simply not true that most people think all things unnatural are bad. That means being unnatural is no reason for homosexuality to be considered wrong. (There is also the question of in what sense homosexuality is supposed to be unnatural.) The second problem is a logical one. Because something "is" the case, it doesn't follow that it "ought" to be the case. "Cancer kills" is true, but that doesn't mean "cancer should (in the moral sense of the word) kill." So there is a problem in trying to derive matters of moral value directly from matters of pure fact.

Tension 11: Is positive discrimination justified?

This was the least common tension in the beliefs of our respondents, with less than one in ten having it. The tension emerges only if you agree that *In certain circumstances, it might be desirable to discriminate positively in favor of a person as recompense for harms done to him/her in the past* and disagree that *It is not always right to judge individuals solely on their merits.*

Positive discrimination means that factors other than the actual abilities of a person are taken into account when deciding how to treat them. This means that, under positive discrimination measures, people are not judged solely on their merits. So in order to support positive discrimination, you have to accept that it is sometimes right not to judge individuals on their merits. Alternatively, if you want to maintain that individuals must always be judged on their merits, you must give up your belief in positive discrimination. More sophisticated responses to this tension might include the idea that people should be judged not according to their actual merits but according to the merits they would have if everyone had been given the same opportunities. One problem with this is that it is very difficult to judge what these merits would have been.

Tension 12: What is the seat of the self?

If you agree that *Severe brain damage can rob a person of all consciousness and selfhood* and also that *On bodily death, a person con-*

tinues to exist in a nonphysical form, there's a tension in your beliefs, one you share with nearly one in three of our respondents.

These two beliefs are not strictly contradictory, but they do present an awkward mix of world views. On the one hand, there is an acceptance that our consciousness and sense of self are in some way dependent on brain activity, and this is why brain damage can in a real sense damage "the self." Yet there is also the belief that the self is somehow independent of the body, that it can live on after the death of the brain. So it seems consciousness and selfhood both are and are not dependent on having a healthy brain. One could argue that the dependency of the self on the brain only occurs before bodily death. The deeper problem is not that it is impossible to reconcile the two beliefs, but rather that they seem to presume wider, contradictory world views: one in which consciousness is caused by brains and one in which it is caused by something nonphysical.

Tension 13: What is faith?

This tension arises when someone disagrees that *It is quite reasonable to believe in the existence of a thing without even the possibility of evidence for its existence* but agrees that *Atheism is a faith just like any other, because it is not possible to prove the nonexistence of God*. This tension was found in around a quarter of respondents.

People seem very reluctant to admit this is a real tension, but we think our logic is sound. In disagreeing with the first statement, a person is acting consistently with the general principle that states that in the absence of good grounds for believing something, it is not rational to believe it. For example, it is not possible to disprove the possibility that there are invisible pink fairies at this moment circling the planet Pluto, but we don't countenance it as a real possibility because there is no evidence for their existence. This is not to be thought of as a matter of faith, but of sound reasoning. But asserting that atheism is a faith just like any other, *because* it is not possible to prove the nonexistence of God, contradicts this principle. It replaces the principle "In the absence of good grounds for believing something, it is not rational to believe it" with the principle "In the absence of good grounds for believing something, it requires faith not to believe it." For this reason, atheism is not a matter of faith in the same way as belief in God. In short, belief without evidence (a form of faith) is not the same as nonbelief due to lack of evidence (rational refusal to assent).

Tension 14: How do we judge art?

Nearly half of the people we questioned fell prey to this tension. They did so by agreeing that *Judgments about works of art are purely matters of taste* and also that *Michelangelo is one of history's finest artists*.

The tension here is the result of the fact that most people don't believe the status of Michelangelo is seriously in doubt. One can disagree about who is the best artist of all time, but surely Michelangelo is on the short list. Yet if this is true, how can judgments about works of art be *purely* matters of taste? If someone unskilled were to claim that they were as good an artist as Michelangelo, almost everyone would think that they were wrong, and not just because their tastes differ. They would probably think Michelangelo's superiority to be not just a matter of personal opinion. The tension here is between a belief that works of art can be judged, in certain respects, by some reasonably objective standards and the belief that, nonetheless, the final arbiter of taste is something subjective. This is not a contradiction, but a tension nonetheless.

Tension 15: What should be legal?

This tension is the result of agreeing that *The government should not permit the sale of health treatments that have not been tested for efficacy and safety* and also that *Alternative and complementary medicines are as valuable as mainstream medicine*. A little under half of our respondents had this tension in their beliefs.

The problem here, of course, is that most alternative and complementary medicines have not been tested in trials as rigorously as "conventional" medicine. For example, the popular herbal antidepressant St. John's wort has been found to cause complications when taken alongside any of five other common medicines. This has only come to light because of extensive testing. Yet the product is freely available without medical advice. The question that needs answering here is, why do so many people believe alternative medicines and treatments need not be as extensively tested as conventional ones? The fact that they use natural ingredients is not in itself a good reason, as there are plenty of naturally occurring toxins. Even if one argues that their long history shows them to be safe, that is not the same as showing them to be effective. This is not to criticize alternative therapies, but to question the different standards that are used to judge them compared with mainstream medicines.

Final thoughts

Most people seem quite happy to accept that they're probably not consistent in their opinions and that there may be big holes in the arguments they use. Yet should we be so glib about accepting these failures? We are not so forgiving when it comes to the inconsistencies of governments, for example, branding them hypocrites if one policy runs counter to another.

Perhaps it is simply the case that being reasonably, if not perfectly, consistent is hard work, and we frankly can't be bothered to do it. When you consider that on average we found people had four tensions among this narrow selection of beliefs alone, it seems probable that inconsistency is the norm. Is that something we should be sanguine about, or do we all have a responsibility to think our opinions through much more carefully?

2

So You Think You're Logical?

Man has such a predilection for systems and abstract deductions that he is ready to distort the truth intentionally, he is ready to deny the evidence of his senses only to justify his logic.

Fyodor Dostoevsky

If you find yourself nodding in agreement with Dostoevsky's scathing dismissal of logic, this test may make you think again. Dostoevsky was wrong. Human beings are terrible at logic and are ready to deny the simple evidence of it only to justify their hunches and intuitions.

Yet logic often gets bad press, portrayed as cold, inhuman and irrelevant to the affairs of flesh and blood. "Logic is neither an art nor a science but a dodge," complained Stendhal; "Logic is the art of going wrong with confidence," claimed Joseph Wood Krutch; it is "an instrument for bolstering a prejudice," said Elbert Hubbard. We prefer the unfashionable view expressed by John Locke that "Logic is the anatomy of thought." At least that's the way it should be. But, as you'll soon find out, that's not the way it usually is.

Take the tests

This test consists of four reasoning tasks. You should do them in order, reading the instructions carefully, not proceeding to the next task until you have completed the one before it.

Task 1: Even Vowels

Imagine that you are employed in quality control by a card manufacturer. They are producing a series of cards for an experimental psychologist, according to the following rule: if a card has a vowel on one side, then it has an even number on the other side.

There are four of these cards below. You know for certain that each card has a letter on one side and a number on the other. In light of this knowledge, tick the box(es) under the card or cards you *definitely* need to turn over, and *only that or those cards*, in order to determine whether the rule is broken in the case of any of these four cards.

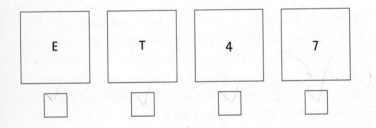

Task 2: Colored Circles and Squares

Imagine that you have been employed by a board games manufacturer to ensure that the cards in one of their games have been correctly produced.

The rule governing the production of the cards states that if a card has a circle on one side, then it has the color yellow on the other.

There are four such cards below. You know for certain that each card has a shape on one side and a color on the other. In light of this knowledge, tick the box(es) under the card or cards you *definitely* need to turn over, and *only that or those cards*, in order to determine whether the rule is broken in the case of any of these four cards.

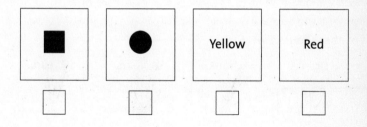

Task 3: Sly Beer Drinking

You are the owner of a bar and you are very concerned that underage-drinking laws should be correctly enforced. Your bar is situated in a university town, and you suspect that some of your clientele might be students not yet old enough to drink legally. At present, the law states that if a person drinks an alcoholic drink (e.g., beer), then they must be more than 21 years old.

The cards below have information about the ages and drinking habits of four of the customers at your bar. Each card represents one person. One side of a card details the age of the person. The other side of the card indicates what they have been drinking.

In light of this knowledge, tick the box(es) under the card or cards you *definitely* need to turn over, and *only that or those cards*, in order to determine whether the rule is broken in the case of any of these four drinkers.

Drank beer	Drank cola	23 years old	19 years old
☐	☐	☐	☐

Task 4: Surfing at Work

Imagine that you are the owner of a small company employing some twenty people. You have noticed that your employees seem to be spending a lot of time during work hours surfing the Web for personal pleasure. You consider this practice to be a perk rather than a right, so you have introduced a rule that states that if an employee spends more than two hours a day during work time on the Web, then they must have made at least $5K for the company in the last month.

The cards below have information about the Web-surfing habits of four of your employees. Each card represents one employee. One side of the card details how much time the employee has spent on the Web during the last working day. The other side details how much money they have made for the company in the last month.

In light of this knowledge, tick the box(es) under the card or cards that you *definitely* need to turn over, and *only that or those cards*, in order to determine whether the rule is broken in the case of any of these four employees.

Spent 1 hour on the Web	Spent 3 hours on the Web	Made $3K last month	Made $7K last month
☐	☐	☐	☐

How did you score?

These are the correct answers.

Task 1	You should have ticked "E" and "7" only
Task 2	You should have ticked "●" and "Red" only
Task 3	You should have ticked "Drank beer" and "19 years old" only
Task 4	You should have ticked "Spent 3 hours on the Web" and "Made $3K last month" only

So what does your score say about you?

0 correct	Go to the bottom of the logic class
1 correct	Could do better
2 correct	You're in the company of around three-quarters of the human race
3 correct	You're what people describe as too clever for your own good
4 correct	You are so logical that people tend to stare at your ears and call you Mr. Spock

For the somewhat subtler reasoning behind these crude head-lines, read on . . .

General analysis

The curious thing about these tests is that the raw logic of each of the four tasks is the same. When we ran these tests online, the first task was completed correctly only 16% of the time, and the second on only 12% of occasions. However, 76% got Task 3 right, and 68% successfully completed Task 4. The same logic, yet totally different success rates. What's going on?

The tasks are variations on one that was devised in 1966 by psychologist Peter Wason. The Wason selection task was originally developed as a test of logical reasoning, but it has increasingly been used by psychologists to analyze the structure of human reasoning mechanisms. It tests the ability of subjects to look for exceptions to a conditional rule of the form "If P, then Q." As you have seen, the task begins with a person being presented with four cards: one card represents P (e.g., a circle); one not-P (e.g., a square); one Q (e.g., yellow); and the other not-Q (e.g., red).

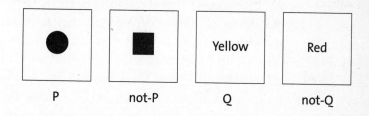

They are told that if there is a shape on one side of the card, then there is a color on the other. The person is then asked to name which of the four cards must definitely be picked up in order to determine whether any of the cards break the rule "If P, then Q"—in this instance: if a card has a circle on one side (P), then it has the color yellow (Q) on the other side.

The answer is that you should pick up the cards with the circle (P) and the color red (not-Q). The card with the square (not-P) does not have to be picked up, as finding a surface of any color on the other side tells us nothing about the truth or falsity of the rule (because the rule says nothing about not-P). And neither does the card with the color yellow showing have to be picked up, because finding a circle or square on the other side of that card would also be uninformative in terms of the rule (it will be obvious that finding a circle on the other side does not falsify the rule, but crucially nor does finding a square, since the rule does NOT say, "If, *and only if*, a card has a circle on one side, then it has the color yellow on the other side").

The significant point about this test is that we are incredibly bad at it! Typically, some 75%–80% of people get the test wrong. The level of education of the person taking the test doesn't make much difference. Even a training in formal logic seems to make little difference to a person's performance! (Indeed, one of us routinely screws up when presenting the tests in person.) The mistake that we tend to make is fairly standard. People almost always recognize that they have to pick up the card with the circle (P), but they fail to see that they also have to pick up the card with the color red (not-Q). And often—and mistakenly—they think instead that they have to pick up the card with the color yellow (Q). One of the most interesting things about this phenomenon is that even when the correct answer is pointed out, people feel resistance to it. It apparently feels "right" that the card with the color yellow (Q) should be picked up.

There are a number of important implications of the fact that we tend to be bad at the Wason selection task and others like it. One has to do with the notion of justified belief. If a belief is recognized to be based on defective reasoning, then to continue to believe it is not justified. But if we systematically, and unconsciously, reason badly, then the extent to which reason actually acts as a constraint on belief is a moot point.

Another implication has to do with what these tests suggest about the way that the human mind has evolved. According to Leda Cosmides and John Tooby, the results of the Wason selection task demonstrate that the human mind has not evolved reasoning procedures that are specialized for detecting logical violations of conditional rules. Moreover, they claim that this is the case even when these rules deal with familiar content drawn from everyday life. However, they argue that the human mind has evolved to detect violations of conditional rules, when these violations involve cheating on a social exchange. This is a situation in which a person is entitled to some kind of reward only if they have fulfilled a particular requirement (e.g., "If a student eats cookies, then their room must be tidy"). Cheating involves taking the benefit without fulfilling the condition for the benefit. It is Cosmides and Tooby's finding that when the Wason selection task is constructed to reflect a cheating scenario, subjects perform considerably better than they do with the standard test. Moreover, they found that this is not simply to do with the familiarity of cheating scenarios—subjects do better with an unfamiliar cheating scenario than they do with a familiar standard scenario.

The tasks that you have just completed have been designed to test these claims. The first two tasks were of the form of a standard Wason selection task. The other two were of the form of a Wason selection task with a cheating context.

If Leda Cosmides and John Tooby are right, and this particular experimental design is sound, then the chances are that you will have found the first two tasks much harder than the last two. In fact, for the tasks with a cheating context, you might well have experienced what Cosmides and Tooby call a "pop out" effect. That is, the correct answer will have appeared to be immediately obvious to you (i.e., it wouldn't have required analysis).

This certainly seems to be what has happened with the thousands who have taken the tests online, since success rates for the non-cheating tasks are very low, whereas most people get the cheating-context tasks right.

The right answers explained

Here's an explanation for what you need to do with each card, so you can see where and why you went wrong—if you did.

Task 1: Even Vowels

Rule: if a card has a vowel on one side, then it has an even number on the other side.

> *Does the card definitely have to be turned over to determine if the rule has been broken in any of the cases represented by these cards?*

"E" Card   Yes. This card has a vowel on one side. It might not have an even number on the other side. It is necessary to turn over the card to determine whether this is the case. If it is, then the rule is broken.

"T" Card   No. The rule says nothing about what must appear on the other side of a card with a consonant. Therefore, there is no need to turn over this card to determine that the rule is not broken.

"4" Card   No. In this instance, the rule is not broken whatever the letter on the other side, so there is no need to turn over the card. In other words, the fact that there is an even number on one side of the card is enough to determine that the rule is not violated, regardless of what appears on the other side.

"7" Card   Yes. The number 7, an odd number, appears on one side of the card. It is possible that the letter on the other side is a vowel. It is necessary to turn over the card to find out whether this is the case. If it is, then the rule is broken.

Task 2: Colored Circles and Squares

Rule: if a card has a circle on one side, then it has the color yellow on the other.

> *Does the card definitely have to be turned over to determine if the rule has been broken in any of the cases represented by these cards?*

"Square" Card   No. The rule says nothing about the color that must appear on the other side of a square. Therefore, there is no need to turn over this card to determine that the rule is not broken.

"Circle" Card   Yes. This card has a circle on one side. It might not have the color yellow on the other. It is necessary to turn over the card to determine whether this is the case. If it is, then the rule is broken.

"Yellow" Card   No. In this instance, the rule is not broken whether there is a circle on the other side or not, so there is no need to turn over the card. In other words, the fact that there is yellow on one side of the card is enough to determine that the rule is not violated, regardless of the shape that appears on the other side.

"Red"   Yes. Red appears on one side of the card. It is possible
Card   that there is a circle on the other side. It is necessary
              to turn over the card to find out whether this is the
              case. If it is, then the rule is broken.

Task 3: Sly Beer Drinking

Rule: if a person drinks an alcoholic drink (e.g., beer), then
they must be more than 21 years old.

> *Does the card definitely have to be turned over
> to determine if the rule has been broken in any
> of the cases represented by these cards?*

"Drank beer"   Yes. The person drank beer. It might be that they
Card   are under 21 years old. It is necessary to turn
                   over the card to find out whether this is the
                   case. If it is, then the rule is broken.

"Drank cola"   No. The rule says nothing about how old people
Card   have to be to drink cola. Therefore, there is no
                   need to turn over this card to determine that
                   the rule is not broken.

"23 years old" No. In this instance, the rule is not broken
Card   whether the person drinks an alcoholic drink or
                    not. In other words, the fact that the drinker is
                    23 years old is enough to determine that the
                    rule is not violated, regardless of what they
                    drink.

"19 years old" Card   Yes. The person is 19. They might be drinking an alcoholic drink. It is necessary to turn over the card to determine whether this is the case. If it is, then the rule is broken.

Task 4: Surfing at Work

Rule: if an employee spends more than two hours a day during work time on the Web, then they must have made at least $5K for the company in the last month.

Does the card definitely have to be turned over to determine if the rule has been broken in any of the cases represented by these cards?

"Spent 1 hour on the Web" Card   No. The rule only refers to employees who spend more than two hours a day during work time on the Web. This person spent only one hour on the Web. Therefore, there is no need to turn over this card to determine that the rule is not broken.

"Spent 3 hours on the Web" Card   Yes. This person spent three hours on the Web. It is possible that they made less than $5K for the company in the last month. It is necessary to turn over the card to find out whether this is the case. If it is, then the rule is broken.

"Made $3K last month" Card   Yes. This person made only $3K for the company last month. It is possible that they spent more than two hours on the Web during the last working day. It is necessary to turn over the card to find out whether this is the case. If it is, then the rule is broken.

"Made $7K last month" Card — No. In this instance, the rule is not broken whether or not the person spent more than two hours during the last working day on the Web. In other words, the fact that they made more than $5K for the company in the preceding month is enough to determine that the rule is not violated, regardless of how long they spent on the Web during working hours.

Final thoughts

People respond in varying ways to the idea that thinking logically is not a very natural thing for human beings to do. For those who value rationality and reason, it's somewhat dispiriting. For others who like to celebrate the irrational and intuitive, it can seem to offer a vindication that reason is not the way forward. But they need to be careful. The fact that something is natural or unnatural does not show it to be right. It may, for example, be quite natural for men to want to inseminate as many women as possible, but it is not necessarily right that they should seek to do so.

What these tests really show is that we need to be aware that our powers of deduction are not as good as we like to think they are, and that we often reach conclusions on the basis of evolved instincts rather than rational thought. It's a warning we should all heed.

3

The Syllogymnasium

It is simplicity that makes the uneducated more effective than the educated when addressing popular audiences.

Aristotle

Aristotle was the founder of formal logic. Yet he knew just how weak it could be when it comes to persuading people. Properly reasoned arguments are often hard to follow, while poorly reasoned ones often work by being emotive and appealing to people's prejudices.

Yet the formal logic Aristotle developed was in principle quite simple. If you pay close attention to it, you should be able to avoid error quite easily. Or so you might think . . .

Warming up in the syllogymnasium

Before you begin your task, we need to explain the rules. These come from a form of argument known as the syllogism, which Aristotle formalized. All you need to know to take our test is one principle, the principle of validity. This states:

An argument is valid *if and only if* the conclusion necessarily follows from the premises.

Here's the most famous example:

41

All men are mortal.
Socrates is a man.
Therefore Socrates is mortal.

It's easy to distinguish the premises from the conclusion: the conclusion comes last and has "therefore" in front of it. The premises provide the basis for reaching this conclusion. This argument is valid because the conclusion follows from the premises. If all men are mortal and Socrates is a man, then it must be the case that Socrates is mortal.

We really need to stress here that validity is solely to do with whether the conclusion *follows*. It has nothing at all to do with the truth of the premises or the conclusion. For example:

All cheese is from the moon.
Chocolate is a cheese.
Therefore chocolate is from the moon.

Cheese isn't from the moon and chocolate isn't cheese, but nevertheless this argument is valid. Why? Because if it were true that all cheese is from the moon and that chocolate is a cheese, it would follow more surely than night follows day that chocolate is from the moon.

Now consider this example:

Vegetarians don't eat pork sausages.
Moby doesn't eat pork sausages.
Therefore Moby is a vegetarian.

The two premises are in fact true and Moby is also a vegetarian, but the argument is invalid because the conclusion does not follow from the premises. For all the premises show,

Moby could be, say, a carnivorous Jew (in other words, he might avoid sausages for reasons that have nothing to do with vegetarianism).

Be prepared for the fact that sometimes the premises may contain a conditional "if" sentence:

If today is Tuesday, then I should be at work.
Today is Tuesday.
Therefore I should be at work.

That is also a valid argument.

That really is all the information you need to take the test. You will be asked to assess validity and this is simply a matter of saying whether the conclusion follows from the premises. You can do that, surely?

Time to work out

So, here's your test. There are ten arguments to assess. All you have to do is to say whether each one is valid or invalid. It is valid if the conclusion follows from the premises; invalid if it does not. It does not matter whether the statements are true or false: it is solely a matter of what follows.

1 If man-made global warming is really happening, then the polar ice caps will be melting.
The polar ice caps are melting.
Therefore man-made global warming is really happening.

2 If acupuncture tended to make people ill, then it would be foolish to try it.
Acupuncture does not tend to make people ill.
Therefore it is not foolish to try it.

3 If I don't get home by six, I'll miss the news.
Therefore, if I get home by six, I won't miss the news.

4 If I work hard, I'll pass my exams.
Therefore, if I don't work hard, I won't pass my exams.

5 All men are bastards.
Some bastards are attractive.
Therefore some men are attractive.

6 All politicians are liars.
No person of integrity is a politician.
Therefore no person of integrity is a liar.

7 All human life is sacred.
All God's creation is sacred.
Therefore all human life is God's creation.

8 Every person is a child of the universe.
Every person is a being of light and hope.
Therefore every being of light and hope is a child of the universe.

9 No vegans are fish eaters.
Some fish eaters are not vegetarians.
Therefore some vegetarians are not vegans.

10 Today isn't both sunny and cold.
Today isn't sunny.
Therefore today is cold.

How did you shape up?

This is easy: every one of the ten syllogisms is invalid. And this is what your score means:

0 mistakes   You are a natural-born logician, or else you've studied this stuff before.

1 & 2 mistakes   To err is human. But you have the potential to become inhumanly logical.

3 & 4 mistakes   You're no fool, but you really need to pay more attention! Try omega-3 oils.

5 & 6 mistakes   Your mind is as slack as the trousers of a man who has just lost twenty pounds and not bought any new clothes.

7+ mistakes   Complete this syllogism. People who make more than six mistakes aren't thinking straight. You made more than six mistakes. Therefore? Oh dear—we've lost you again.

Explaining the mistakes

Every one of our syllogisms is invalid and is an example of a particular type of logical error. But if you read and digest these explanations, you should be better equipped to avoid making these mistakes in the future.

1 *Affirming the consequent*

If man-made global warming is really happening, then the polar ice caps will be melting.

The polar ice caps are melting.
Therefore man-made global warming is really happening.

As with all syllogisms, we can describe the general form of the argument by replacing the specific content with letters. So the first thing to do is to identify the specific content:

If [man-made global warming is really happening], then [the polar ice caps will be melting].
[The polar ice caps are melting].
Therefore [man-made global warming is really happening].

Notice that there are only two different pieces of specific content, or "terms." These are:

Man-made global warming is really happening.
The polar ice caps are melting.

Substitute all instances of the former with p and of the latter with q and you have the general form of this argument.

If p then q
q
Then p

Stripped down to its bare form, it is now easier to see whether this is a valid argumentative form or not. If it is, then any argument of this form in which the premises are true will generate a true conclusion. But consider this example:

If it's Monday, the banks will be open.
The banks are open.
Therefore it's Monday.

Clearly the conclusion doesn't follow. The reason is that banks are open on days other than Monday too, so although we can know that if it's Monday, the banks will be open, we cannot be sure it's Monday just because the banks are open. The conditional cannot be reversed.

However, this bogus logic is something many often fall for. One reason has to do with an ambiguity in language. We sometimes say "if" and we mean "if and only if." When a parent says they will treat their kids if they work hard, the implication is that they won't treat them if they don't. The "if" here means "if and only if." But most "ifs" are not like this. If you win the lottery, you might go on a cruise. But you might go on a cruise even if you don't win.

In the global warming example the difference is crucial. All sorts of things will happen if global warming is real and manmade. But some of these might also happen even if the planet isn't heating up. The "ifs" in this case are even bigger than usual.

2 *Denying the antecedent*

If acupuncture tended to make people ill, then it would be foolish to try it.
Acupuncture does not tend to make people ill.
Therefore it is not foolish to try it.

The form of this argument is:

If p then q.
Not-p.
Therefore not-q.

The form is shared by this example:

> If it's a cat, then it's furry.
> It's not a cat.
> Therefore it isn't furry.

Clear nonsense, of course. Cats are not the only furry things. And in the acupuncture example, there *may* be reasons why it is foolish to try it other than the fact that it makes you ill. It could be ineffective, time-consuming and expensive, for example.

3 *Improper transposition (a)*

> If I don't get home by six, I'll miss the news.
> Therefore, if I get home by six, I won't miss the news.

The form of this argument is:

> If not-p then not-q.
> Therefore if p then q.

This is not strictly a syllogism, since a syllogism has two premises and a conclusion. Rather, it is the fundamental error of denying the antecedent laid bare. You can see it is wrong clearly by this counterexample:

> If it's not a dog, then it isn't Lassie.
> Therefore, if it is a dog, it is Lassie.

There are other dogs than Lassie, and there are other reasons for missing the news than getting home late for it.

4 *Improper transposition (b)*

If I work hard, I'll pass my exams.
Therefore, if I don't work hard, I won't pass my exams.

This is the mirror image of the previous example, with positives in the premises changed into negatives in the conclusion, rather than vice versa. Again, a simple counterexample will expose the flaw in the logic.

If I stay up all night, I'll be able to watch the sunrise.
If I don't stay up all night, I won't be able to watch the sunrise.

But there are other ways to catch the sunrise, such as getting up early. Again, one potential source of the mistake is a confusion of "if" with "if and only if."

5 *Some/all confusion*

All men are bastards.
Some bastards are attractive.
Therefore some men are attractive.

This shares the same form (no need to spell it out now, surely) as:

All cows are four-legged animals.
Some four-legged animals are elephants.
Therefore some cows are elephants.

Doesn't work, does it?

6 *Illicit major*

All politicians are liars.
No person of integrity is a politician.
Therefore no person of integrity is a liar.

Right, so likewise:

All Catholics are Christians.
No Methodists are Catholics.
Therefore no Methodists are Christians.

There are some who would agree with the conclusion, but the logic that leads to it is clearly faulty.

7 *Undistributed middle*

All human life is sacred.
All God's creation is sacred.
Therefore all human life is God's creation.

By the same logic . . .

All champagne is made from grapes.
All liebfraumilch is made from grapes.
Therefore all champagne is liebfraumilch.

Try that one on your party guests.

8 *Illicit minor*

Every person is a child of the universe.
Every person is a being of light and hope.

51

Therefore every being of light and hope is a child of the universe.

And likewise:

Every cow is a mammal.
Every cow is a four-legged creature.
Therefore every four-legged creature is a mammal.

You should never teach logic to a crocodile.

9 Exclusive premises

No vegans are fish eaters.
Some fish eaters are not vegetarians.
Therefore some vegetarians are not vegans.

Compare this with . . .

No mammals are chickens.
Some chickens are not elephants.
Therefore some elephants are not mammals.

This one can actually be a little baffling. The trouble is that the second premise sounds wrong. Why say "some fish eaters are not vegetarians": surely no fish eaters are vegetarians, just as no chickens are elephants, not just some. But from a logical point of view, if no chickens are elephants, it must also be true that some aren't. To say that some things are x does not rule out the possibility that, in fact, all are. To be strictly logical, you should never say "some are not" when you mean "none are." Pedantic? Yes, but logic demands precision.

10 *Denying a conjunct*

> Today isn't both sunny and cold.
> Today isn't sunny.
> Therefore today is cold.

Another one in which ordinary speech glosses over logical imprecision. Consider:

> England isn't both bigger than America and hotter than
> Jamaica.
> England isn't bigger than America.
> Therefore it's hotter than Jamaica.

The logical point is that if something is not both one thing and another, it could still be neither. But when we say "it's not both" we often mean to imply that it is nonetheless one of the two things on offer. Logic, however, has no time for such ambiguity!

Final thoughts

In some of these examples, logic seems rather alien and irrelevant. We often know what we mean in everyday speech, and the pedantry of the logician seems inappropriate. Furthermore, validity has nothing to do with whether premises are true. So what is the use of it?

The use is that sound arguments—*sound* actually being the right technical term—are ones that are both valid and have true premises, and therefore also true conclusions. Sound arguments therefore require two things: true premises and valid inferences. Finding out whether premises are true is one skill, while working out whether arguments are valid is another.

Logic focuses on the second not for its own sake but because it is an essential part of good reasoning.

Logic is not just for nerds, because in ordinary language we are often misled by our failure to attend properly to the logic of arguments. Most noticeably, we infer all sorts of incorrect things from what we believe follows from "if" statements. That's probably why so many effective speeches use conditionals: "If you want a better country, vote for me" does not logically imply that if you don't vote for her you don't want a better country, but that's how you're made to feel.

Most of us are not natural logicians, so we need not fear being turned into heartless automatons by trying harder to think about the validity of the arguments we hear and offer. What we might gain by doing so, however, is some protection against making mistakes that lead us to embrace false conclusions.

4

The Do-It-Yourself Deity

> I do not feel obliged to believe that the same God who has
> endowed us with sense, reason and intellect has intended us
> to forgo their use.
>
> Galileo Galilei

Do you believe in God? Your answer is meaningful only if we know what kind of God you do or don't believe in. It makes a big difference whether your God is a vengeful despot who demands obedience, a loving father, an impersonal force of nature or perhaps just nature itself. Indeed, unless we know what exactly we mean when we say "God," we can't really understand any other statement we make about him (or her).

But how easy is it to specify what we mean by God, even in general terms? Does God become more real the fuller our definition of him, or does he become more and more mysterious? With the help of our metaphysical engineers, trained in the craft of God-building, we're about to find out.

Build your God

What do *you* mean by "God"? Listed below are eight attributes that any being that claims to be divine might have. All you need to do is select which ones your God has.

If you believe in God, then you should try to pick the attributes you think this deity has. If you don't, then pick the attributes of the being you don't believe in but you think most believers do!

This list comprises characteristics of deities in the Abrahamic traditions. If your God is far removed from this, or if you think God can't be said to have any of these characteristics, then you could try the exercise by selecting the attributes you think someone who belongs to this tradition might believe in.

Choose as many, or as few, attributes as you wish.

☑ 1 Omnipotent (all-powerful, able to do anything)

☐ 2 Omnibenevolent (all-loving)

☑ 3 Omniscient (all-knowing)

☐ 4 The Creator

☐ 5 The Sustainer of All That Exists (i.e., if God ceased to exist, so would everything else)

☐ 6 Perfectly Free

☐ 7 Eternally Existing

☑ 8 A Personal God (a being with whom one can have a personal relationship)

How does your God shape up?

To analyze your deity, you need to do the following:

1   Shade in every box opposite that has the number of the attribute you gave to your God. (Note that a box might not be a regular shape. Box 1 is L-shaped, for example.)

2   Also shade in the "any 2 of 1–7" or "2 or fewer attributes chosen" if they apply to you.

3   If the area to the left of any letter A–H is now completely shaded, then tick the box to the right of the letter in the Alert! column. For example, if you shaded boxes 1, 2 and 3, then the line to the left of B will be completely shaded, so you should tick the Alert! column next to B. The description in the Technical difficulty column describes this alert and will be explained more fully in the analysis that follows.

4   In the Alerts total box at the bottom of the Alert! column, write in the total number of ticks in that column.

				Alert!	Technical difficulty
			4	A	Why this universe?
	2	3		B	The problem of suffering
		6		C	The problem of loving too much
1				D	Doing the impossible
5				E	The redundant sustainer
7				F	Infinite problems
8	any 2 of 1–7			G	Not so personal after all?
2 or fewer attributes chosen				H	The empty word
Alerts total					

Your design for a deity has been tested against the criteria set out by our metaphysical engineers. Their full report will follow, but here are their headline findings.

0 Alerts   Congratulations! There is no logical reason why our metaphysical engineers can't construct your God—which isn't to say one actually has been built.

1 & 2 Alerts   In our universe, it may be tricky to build your God, but if you manage to iron out a few wrinkles in your concept of the deity, it should be possible.

3 & 4 Alerts Constructing your God faces huge logical difficulties, ones the metaphysical engineers cannot overcome. Indeed, they suspect no one could manage to build it.

5+ Alerts Your blueprint for God is a logical mess. Maybe you should consider becoming a mystic?

General analysis

This thought experiment is designed to answer two questions about your conception of God.

1   Is the conception of God consistent with itself?

2   Is the conception of God consistent with the universe that we live in?

The first question asks whether the conception makes sense. For example, a triangle with four sides is a conception that is not consistent with itself, since a triangle by definition has only three sides. A triangle with four sides is, in fact, a four-sided three-sided object, which is simply a contradiction in terms. In this sense, the conception is not consistent with itself.

If a conception is consistent with itself, this does not necessarily mean that it refers to something that actually exists. For example, the idea of a 600-foot monster that lives in liquid steel is not inconsistent. But such a creature does not exist in our world. The second question therefore asks whether your conception of God is consistent with the universe as we understand it.

Together, the answers to these two questions help to indicate the plausibility of your conception of God. This is not an attempt to show that God does or doesn't exist. Rather, it is a look at whether the very idea you have of God makes sense or not.

The more alerts you ticked, the more intellectual barriers there are between your idea of God and conceptual coherence. Of course, these problems are not in any way weighted. A conception of God with one glaring contradiction is more problematic than one that raises several tricky questions.

But what exactly are these barriers? On the score grid, we gave a name for each technical difficulty that the alerts indicate. In the detailed analysis that follows, we turn to our metaphysical engineers to explain what these are.

The Metaphysical Engineers' Report

Our metaphysical engineers have devised a new computer-modeling virtual environment in which to test the plausibility of different conceptions of God. Each technical difficulty describes a problem they have faced when trying to model Gods with certain combinations of attributes.

The problems the metaphysical engineers report may reveal one of two things. Some may simply reflect their inability to resolve *apparent* problems. In this sense, the difficulties are a product of their lack of knowledge or understanding. Others may be deeper problems, so fundamental that no amount of increased understanding can resolve them. It is for you to decide which problems fall into which category.

A *Why this universe?*

We have run up against a problem modeling a God that is omnipotent (all-powerful, able to do anything), omnibenevolent (all-loving), omniscient (all-knowing) and the creator of all that exists. If such a God created the universe, being all-knowing, she must have known about all the suffering there would be in this world. Yet God still created it, as it is. She did not create a more benign version of the universe or simply choose not to create the universe. Why is this?

It could be that God did not know about all the suffering that would occur. But that would make God not all-knowing. It could be that God doesn't mind all the suffering, but that would make her less than all-loving. It could be that God could not have created a more benign world than this one. But that would seem to make God less than all-powerful. The only way we can resolve this problem is to conclude that God can only do what is possible and that this really is the best of all possible worlds. We find it hard to model this resolution, as we think we can make a better world quite easily. For example, we are able to make human brains more emotionally robust and thus reduce the incidence of psychopathology, resulting in an immediate decline, in our model, of crimes of sadistic murder. Are we mistaken in some way?

We are continuing to study theodicies, an area of advanced metaphysical engineering that seeks to resolve this difficulty, known as the problem of evil.

B *The problem of suffering*

We have found it hard to model an omnipotent (all-powerful, able to do anything), omnibenevolent (all-loving) and omniscient (all-knowing) God in a universe like our own. The problem is similar to the one above, but it does not require us to suppose God actually created the world.

Even if God didn't make it, our universe contains vast amounts of suffering, much of which seems either entirely unnecessary or unnecessarily severe. Although some of this is the result of human action, and thus may be seen as an inevitable consequence of human free will, much is not. Plagues, floods and famines are not all the result of human action. Even the idea that human free will explains the existence of much suffering is hard to accept, since God, if all-powerful, could surely limit our capacity to harm others or suffer at their hands (after all, there are many other limits on what we are able to do).

So why is there all this suffering? If God cannot prevent it, it would seem she is not all-powerful. If God doesn't want to stop it, it would seem she is not all-loving. If God doesn't know about it, she can't be all-knowing.

C *The problem of loving too much*

We have confronted a difficulty modeling an omnipotent (all-powerful, able to do anything), omnibenevolent (all-loving) and perfectly free God. If perfectly free, then God could choose whatever she wants. Nothing could stop this because God is omnipotent. But this God is also all-loving. It seems to us that such a God could never choose to do something that is unloving. It is not that God just chooses not to do such things, rather that God's nature as omnibenevolent constrains what she can do. In other words, God does not have the freedom and/or the power to do something unloving.

One possible response is that God isn't necessarily omnibenevolent but, as a matter of fact, since she never chooses to do something that is unloving, is omnibenevolent. However, if this is true, then we can't see how omnibenevolence can be a necessary characteristic of a God.

We suggest that this whole issue may hinge on a problem with our understanding of "a perfectly free agent." Perhaps we find it hard to build a God with this characteristic because it doesn't mean what it seems to mean, namely, that God can choose to do literally anything.

D *Doing the impossible*

We can't model an all-powerful God without some vital clarification of what this means.

In our first model, God was asked to make $2 + 2 = 5$ (where all the terms hold their common meanings). She could not do so and the model broke down. It seems that no being can ever do what is logically impossible. It is not just beyond the wit of humanity to make $2 + 2 = 5$, such a thing is a contradiction in terms.

So we concluded that by "all-powerful" the most we could mean is that God can do anything that is logically possible. But accepting the limits of logical possibility on God, we would leave open the possibility that, if some characteristics we attribute to God turn out to entail logical contradictions, we must give these up. It means, in effect, accepting that rationality is a constraint on God (though it is a moot point exactly what the word *constraint* means in this regard).

E *The redundant sustainer*

Given the way our universe actually is, we found it hard to model a God that is the sustainer of all that is. This would mean the universe would cease to exist if God did. But the laws of physics, which constrain our models, do not seem to require that the universe has anything outside of itself or divine to continue to exist. Therefore, we can't quite see what place a God required for the universe to continue could have in the universe we actually have.

It has been suggested that a divine sustainer is in fact needed: a lawgiver or law-enforcer is required in order to sustain the laws of physics. But this response seems to rest on a misunderstanding of the nature of physical laws. Laws in the legal sense do require lawgivers and law-enforcers. But physical laws are simply descriptions of the nature of reality. So the idea that a lawgiver is needed to sustain the rules of physics seems to confuse the legal and scientific senses of laws.

F *Infinite problems*

We found it difficult to model an infinite God without some clarification of what this means. Does it mean that God exists through all space and time? But according to our best physics, space and time exist only within the confines of a universe. So the concept of a God immanent in all time and space would seem to constrain God's existence to within a universe.

It could mean that God exists "outside" space and time. But we find it hard to understand what "eternally" would mean in this context. Doesn't the concept "eternally" require some notion of time to make sense?

G *Not so personal after all?*

We are finding it hard to understand how one can have a personal relationship with a God that has many of the characteristics of a deity constructed on the template of the Abrahamic God.

Personal relationships appear to depend on a number of things. Sufficient similarity between the persons in the relationship is one. Another is that both are persons or are, at least, person-like, as some higher primates, for example, appear to be. The problem is that in our universe there seem to be no genuine personal relationships between things of great difference. And a God that is all-powerful, all-loving, all-knowing, the creator and sustainer of all things and infinite is vastly different from human beings.

People can have feelings for things that are similar to those they have toward people. Affection or love for places or objects, for example, is common. But this is not the same as having a personal relationship with them. In a similar way, people have relationships with animals, maybe a cat. But this does not seem to be the same as a personal relationship, because of the great difference in the way the person relates to the animal and the animal relates to the person. Is this the kind of thing envisaged by those who claim we can have a relationship with God?

H *The empty word*

You may get around some of the potential contradictions in the concept of God simply by giving it just a couple of attributes. But then you face another problem: isn't this conception too thin to do the job of explaining God? For example, can a God be all-powerful and not also all-knowing? Wouldn't not knowing be a limit on its power? Or what about a God that sustained the universe but didn't create it? Isn't that an odd kind of deity?

We can model some of these minimal Gods, but we don't think that what we come up with much resembles what we think of as God. It's like asking race-car manufacturers to build a bicycle and expecting their drivers to be able to win the Le Mans 24-hour race on it.

Final thoughts

You might think our attempt to "model" God somewhat crass. Haven't we forgotten that God is described as "surpassing human understanding"? Not at all. We know people say this. But in the next breath they are ascribing very particular properties to this previously inscrutable deity.

You can't have your heavenly cake and eat it too. If you believe God cannot be described in human language, then don't speak of him. Or if you do, understand that you are using no more than metaphors, and don't fall into the trap of pretending you know what they mean. That is harder than it sounds. One reason to love God is that God is all-loving. But if you think we really don't know what that means, it isn't clear why God deserves your love, or why you should think of divine love as being anything like its human counterpart.

But if you do think descriptions of God are better than

vague metaphors, you have to take seriously the conceptual difficulties that arise. The trouble is that many people shuttle back and forth between these two options, resorting to the mysterious God only when they confront a problem with their usual non-mysterious understanding of him.

5

Battleground God

Reason is God's crowning gift to man.

Sophocles

In his book *Fear and Trembling*, the nineteenth-century Danish philosopher Søren Kierkegaard dissects the nature of faith. What he comes up with is a far cry from the comfortable idea of faith that is so often preached in churches—hence the disturbing title. For Kierkegaard, faith induces dread because it is not just unsupported by reason but often requires us to go beyond it and embrace the absurd and the contradictory.

But for most people, to describe their beliefs as absurd and contradictory would be an insult. That's why most of us—believers and nonbelievers—tend to think our beliefs about religion are reasonable and consistent. But are they? Battleground God will help you to find out.

Venture across the battleground

Can your beliefs about religion make it across our intellectual battleground unscathed? In this activity you'll be asked to respond to eighteen statements about God and religion. In each case (apart from Question 1, in which "Don't know" is a possible response), you need to answer True or False. You may feel this offers too narrow a choice, and that your belief is not captured by either option. But you should always be able to answer, since if you cannot agree that the statement is true, even if your own belief is close to it, then you should mark it as false. Do not worry about whether a box is shaded or not— this is simply to help with the analysis later and does not indicate a right or wrong answer.

The aim of the activity is not to judge whether these answers are correct or not. Our battleground is that of rational consistency. This means to get across without taking any hits, you'll need to answer in a way that is rationally consistent: you need to avoid choosing answers that contradict each other. If you answer in a way that is rationally consistent but that has strange or unpalatable implications, you'll be forced to "bite a bullet": accept something many find unpalatable and would view as being a major problem.

Of course, you may go along with thinkers such as Kierkegaard and believe that religious belief does not need to be rationally consistent. Whether that is something you should agree with is beyond the scope of this test, which is about the extent to which your beliefs are rationally consistent, not whether this is a good or a bad thing.

Good luck!

	True	False	Don't know
1 God exists.			
2 God is a logical possibility (i.e., there is nothing self-contradictory about the very idea of God).			

	True	False
3 If God does not exist, then there is no basis for morality.		
4 Any being that it is right to call God must be free to do anything.		
5 Any being that it is right to call God must want there to be as little suffering in the world as possible.		
6 Any being that it is right to call God must have the power to do anything.		
7 Evolutionary theory may be false in some matters of detail, but it is essentially true.		
8 It is justifiable to base one's beliefs about the external world on a firm, inner conviction, even in the absence of any external evidence for the truth of these convictions.		
9 Any being that it is right to call God must know everything that there is to know.		
10 Torturing innocent people is morally wrong.		

	True	False
11 If, despite years of trying, no strong evidence or argument has been presented to show that there is a Loch Ness monster, it is rational to believe that such a monster does not exist.	☒	
12 People who die of horrible, painful diseases need to die in such a way for some higher purpose.		☒
13 If God exists, she could make it so that everything now considered sinful becomes morally acceptable and everything that is now considered morally good becomes sinful.	☒	
14 It is foolish to believe in God without certain, irrevocable proof that God exists.	☒	▓
15 As long as there are no compelling arguments or evidence that show that God does not exist, atheism is a matter of faith, not rationality.		▓

	True	False
16 The serial rapist Peter Sutcliffe had a firm, inner conviction that God wanted him to rape and murder prostitutes. He was, therefore, justified in believing that he was carrying out God's will in undertaking these actions.		✗
17 If God exists, she could create square circles and make $1 + 1 = 72$.	✗	
18 It is justifiable to believe in God if one has a firm, inner conviction that God exists, even if there is no external evidence that God exists.		✗

How did you score?

The scoring of this game looks more complicated than that of some others, but it's not as daunting as you might think!

In your answer grid, you can ignore any answers in the shaded boxes. For all the others, you need to find the box that corresponds to each of your answers on the diagram opposite.

Then:

1 Shade all boxes that correspond to the answers you gave in the scoring grid. If, for example, you answered True to 14, you should shade in the whole box—which has two parts linked by a thin stem. But don't shade the stem itself as that makes reading the chart harder.

2 Now see if any of the arrows pass only through boxes that are all shaded. For example, take the first arrow. If you answered True to 3 and 4 and False to 13, then you've suffered from Hit 6. Put a tick next to it. That's just one hit, not six of them—the number will tell you which analysis to look at to explain why it is a hit.

3 On three occasions, it is possible you need to answer a tie-breaker in order to determine whether you've taken a hit or bitten a bullet. These are printed on the following page.

4 When you've identified your hits and bullets, for each bullet score 1 point and for every direct hit score 3 points.

5 See what your score means.

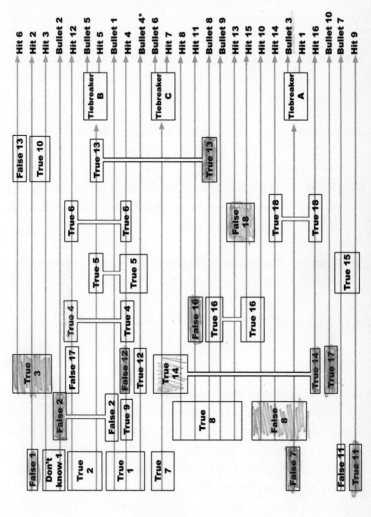

*Only if you have also answered True to one or more of 4, 6 or 9
A larger version of this diagram can be downloaded from www.doyouthinkwhatyouthink.com

75

0 points Congratulations! You are among the fewer than 10% of people to emerge from this battlefield completely unscathed. You are a model of consistency.

1–3 points You're just irrational enough to appear human without losing claim to a large, dominating intellect.

4 & 5 points You're more consistent than the average, but from a rational point of view you're somewhat imperfect.

6–10 points Your ideas about God and religion are not clear and consistent enough for our liking, but you seem redeemable!

11+ points You haven't thought this subject through at all, have you?

The tiebreakers

Tiebreaker A

You don't think that it is justifiable to base one's beliefs about the external world on a firm, inner conviction, paying no regard to the external evidence, or lack of it, for the truth or falsity of this conviction. But you also rejected evolutionary theory when the vast majority of scientists think both that the evidence points to its truth and that there is no evidence that falsifies it. Of course, many creationists claim that the evidential case for evolution is by no means conclusive. But in doing so, they go against scientific orthodoxy. So you've got to make a choice: (a) bite the bullet and say there is evidence that evolution is not true, despite what the scientists say; (b) take a direct hit and say that this is an area in which your beliefs are in contradiction.

Tiebreaker B

You claimed that any being that it is right to call God must want there to be as little suffering in the world as possible. But you also say that God could make it so that everything now considered sinful becomes morally acceptable and everything that is now considered morally good becomes sinful. What this means is that God could make the reduction of suffering a sin . . . yet you've said that God must want to reduce suffering. There is a way out of this, but it means biting a bullet. So you've got to make a choice: (a) bite the bullet and say that it is possible that God wants what is sinful (to reiterate the argument here—she must want to reduce suffering; she could make the reduction of suffering a sin; but if she did so, what she wanted [reducing suffering] would be sinful); (b) take a direct hit and say that this is an area in which your beliefs are in contradiction.

Tiebreaker C

You stated that evolutionary theory is essentially true. However, you also claimed that it is foolish to believe in God without certain, irrevocable proof that she exists. The problem is that there is no certain proof that evolutionary theory is true—even though there is overwhelming evidence that it is true. So it seems that you require certain, irrevocable proof for God's existence but accept evolutionary theory without certain proof. So you've got a choice: (a) bite the bullet and claim that a higher standard of proof is required for belief in

God than for belief in evolution; (b) take a direct hit, conceding that there is a contradiction in your responses.

The rules of engagement

The aim of the game was to get across the intellectual battleground unscathed. There are two types of injury you could have received.

A direct hit occurred when you answered in a way that implies a logical contradiction. We have been very careful to make sure that only strict contradictions result in a direct hit. However, we do make two caveats.

First, because you only had choices between preselected and carefully worded statements, you might find that you have taken a direct hit because the statement closer to your own conviction leads into a contradiction. However, had you phrased the statement yourself, you may have been able to avoid the contradiction while expressing a very similar belief.

Such possibilities are unavoidable given the constraints on the game. So do not take it personally if you suffered a direct hit, and don't get too frustrated if the choices we offered you sometimes forced you into a choice you'd rather not have made.

You had to bite a bullet if your choices had an implication that most would find strange, incredible or unpalatable. There is more room for disagreement here, since what strikes many people as extraordinary or bizarre can strike others as normal. So, again, please don't get too upset if we judge you have bitten a bullet. Maybe it is our world view that is warped!

We have run a version of this game online for a long time and have been inundated with replies from people claiming we're wrong, stupid, evil or destined for hell. Because you, too, may be thinking some of these things right now, before looking at the detailed analysis it's worth addressing some of the most frequently asked questions. This should help explain the rationale of the game better.

One thing we often hear is that the activity is just an exercise to trap religious believers. But this simply isn't true. Only three out of the twenty-six hits and bullets require a True response to the proposition that "God exists."

Another common source of indignation is the apparently frivolous reference to Nessie, the Loch Ness monster. This comparison is often misunderstood, since it is thought we are trying to suggest belief in God is as silly as belief in the Loch Ness monster. But this is not our point at all. What we're trying to do is to establish what the reasonable grounds are for belief or nonbelief in *anything*.

The statement about the Loch Ness monster is, "If, despite years of trying, no strong evidence or argument has been presented to show that there is a Loch Ness monster, it is rational to believe that such a monster does not exist."

If you agree with this you are in effect saying that sometimes—despite the popular maxim to the contrary—absence of evidence is evidence of absence. In other words, it can be reasonable to believe that something does not exist even if you can't prove it doesn't exist. In fact, we do this all the time, when there is no evidence to be found where the evidence would be found if that thing really existed.

But this contradicts the principle behind statement 15: "As long as there are no compelling arguments or evidence that show that God does not exist, atheism is a matter of faith, not rationality." This endorses the contrary view that absence of evidence is not evidence of absence and that until you prove something does not exist, it is mere faith to believe it doesn't. But on this principle, nonbelief in the Loch Ness monster is also a matter of faith and not something it is rational to believe.

Of course, you may think Nessie and God are very different types of being, but that is beside the point. We are not saying that the case against God is as firm as the case against Nessie. Our point is not about the strength of the case for or against God's existence. It is rather about the principles upon which these cases are made. Our "gotchas" show an inconsistency in the principles used; they do not say anything about the probability or otherwise of God's existence.

We also hear from people who quote theologians and philosophers of religion such as Plantinga and Tillich. The point they make is that there are some very sophisticated ways of understanding these issues that may enable evasion of the various bullets. This may be true, but our reply is simply that this activity is not aimed at high-level theologians. The fact that someone has studied these issues for decades and has a very clever reply is interesting, but if you can't offer these replies yourself, you have indeed been caught out. And if you can offer them, well done! We never claimed this activity was the last word.

It is still possible that we've made obvious logical errors and missed certain "get-outs." But in our experience, the vast majority of complaints we receive have just missed the point. We would boldly claim that if you think the test makes an obvious error, you're wrong!

Detailed analysis

Here we explain every direct hit or bitten bullet. You can just look up the ones you have suffered, but you may also find it interesting to discover what the other "gotchas" are and how many people fall for them.

Bullet 1

How can it be claimed that God exists, yet God is a logical impossibility? Indeed, many would claim this is a direct hit, since it is usually held that a logical impossibility cannot exist. But we would rather say this view requires biting a nasty bullet, for if you really believe logical impossibilities can exist, what criteria can you use to determine whether anything in this world is possible or not?

Bullet 2

It is strange to say that God is a logical impossibility, but you don't know whether God exists. If God is a logical impossibility, then surely she can't exist, and so you know that she doesn't exist. See Bullet 1 for more on the rationale behind this.

Bullet 3

If you don't think that it is justifiable to base one's beliefs about the external world on a firm, inner conviction, paying no regard to the external evidence, or lack of it, for the truth or falsity of this conviction, then how can you reject evolutionary theory when the vast majority of scientists think both that the evidence points to its truth and that there is no evidence that falsifies it? Of course, many creationists claim that the evidential case for evolution is by no means conclusive. But in doing so, they go against the vast weight of scientific opinion. To bite the bullet in this case is therefore to say there is evidence that evolution is not true, despite what the scientists say. About one person in twenty bite this bullet.

Hit 1

This hit is suffered when you refuse to bite Bullet 3 (see previous page) and just accept that this is an area in which your beliefs are in contradiction. Only about 2% of people take this hit.

Hit 2

If you say that God doesn't exist and you also say that if she does not exist there is no basis for morality, you are committed to the view that there is no basis for morality. That means if you also say that torturing innocent people is morally wrong, you do so with no basis for morality. Therefore you cannot rationally say of any act that it is morally wrong. You may, of course, say it is wrong for nonrational reasons, but remember this activity is concerned with the rationality of beliefs, which is why, under its rules, you've taken a very rare hit, one suffered by fewer than one in one hundred.

Hit 3

You get hit if you say that you don't know whether God exists, that there is no basis for morality if God does not exist and that torturing innocent people is morally wrong. But if you do not know whether God exists, on your view you do not know whether there is a basis for morality, either. This means you are not rationally entitled to say of any act that it is morally wrong: you should be as agnostic about your moral judgments as you are about your belief in God, since you think that the two go together. Only around 1% of people take this hit.

Hit 4

The claims that God exists, that she knows about suffering, wants to reduce it and can reduce it are not compatible with the claims that there is no higher purpose that explains why people die horribly of painful diseases. If there were no such purpose, why would God allow it? Surely, a God that knows about, wants to stop and can stop suffering would put an end to pointless suffering, unless there is a higher purpose to this suffering. Nonetheless, about one in twenty suffer this hit.

Bullet 4

This is a bullet because many people cannot accept that a loving God—a God that possesses great power and insight—has created the world in such a way that people need to suffer horribly for some higher purpose. There is no logical contradiction in this position, but some would argue that it is obscene. Could you really look someone dying of a horrible flesh-eating disease in the eye and tell them that their suffering is for the greater good of themselves or the world? A little more than one in twenty bite this bullet.

Bullet 5

If you think that any being that it is right to call God must want there to be as little suffering in the world as possible, how can you also claim that God could make it so that everything now considered sinful becomes morally acceptable and everything that is now considered morally good becomes sinful? What this means is that God could make the reduction of suffering a sin … yet this would contradict the claim that God must want to reduce suffering.

The way out of this contradiction is to say that it is possible that God could want what is sinful: she must want to reduce suffering but she could also make the reduction of suffering a sin, making what she wanted sinful. About 8% of people are actually willing to bite this bullet.

Hit 5

Faced with the contradiction in Bullet 5 (see previous page), people take a hit if they refuse to bite the bullet offered to them. About one in twenty take this hit.

Hit 6

This hit is a result of claiming that God is the basis of morality and that if God does exist, she cannot make what is sinful good and vice versa. The problem is that if God were the basis of morality, then she could decide what is good and what is bad. But if God cannot make what is sinful good and vice versa, then things must be right or wrong independently of what God decides. In other words, God chooses what is right because it is right; things are not right just because God chooses them. But if that is true, then there is a basis of morality even if God doesn't exist. About 4% of people take this hit.

Bullet 6

This is a bullet that many atheists have to bite. You cannot claim that evolutionary theory is essentially true, and also that it is foolish to believe in God without certain, irrevocable proof that she exists. The problem is that there is no certain proof that evolutionary theory is true—even though there is overwhelming evidence that it is true. How can you consistently require certain, irrevocable proof for God's existence but accept evolutionary theory without certain proof? Well, by biting a bullet and saying a higher standard of proof is required for belief in God than for belief in evolution. But this seems unfairly and unreasonably to vary the burden of proof. Still, over 10% bite this bullet.

Hit 7

This hit, taken by a little under one in twenty, is a consequence of facing the contradiction described in Bullet 6 (see above) but not biting it and so conceding that there is a contradiction in your responses.

Hit 8

This hit is the contradiction between believing *both* that it is justifiable to base one's beliefs about the external world on a firm, inner conviction, regardless of the external evidence, or lack of it, for the truth or falsity of this conviction; *and* that it is foolish to believe in God without certain, irrevocable proof that God exists. But a firm, inner conviction can never be certain proof, since we know that people have firm, inner convictions about things that are false. About 4% take this hit.

Hit 9

One-third of players of this game take this hit, and they don't like it! They agree that it is rational to believe that the Loch

Ness monster does not exist if there is an absence of strong evidence or argument that it does. No strong evidence or argument was required to show that the monster does not exist—absence of evidence or argument was enough. But then they claim that the atheist needs to be able to provide strong arguments or evidence if their belief in the nonexistence of God is to be rational rather than a matter of faith. The contradiction is that on the first occasion (Loch Ness monster) they agree that the absence of evidence or argument is enough to rationally justify belief in the nonexistence of the Loch Ness monster, but on the second occasion (God) they do not.

Bullet 7

You say that if there are no compelling arguments or evidence that show that God does not exist, then atheism is a matter of faith, not rationality. Therefore, you do not think that the mere absence of evidence for the existence of God is enough to justify believing that she does not exist. Fair enough—but what if you also claim that it is not rational to believe that the Loch Ness monster does not exist even if, despite years of trying, no evidence has been presented to suggest that it does exist? There is no logical inconsistency here, but by denying that the absence of evidence, even where it has been sought, is enough to justify belief in the nonexistence of things, you are required to countenance possibilities that most people would find bizarre. For example, would you really want to claim that it is not rationally justified to believe that intelligent aliens do not live on Mars? There's a tricky double negative there, but it is required. The point is that if you hold this view on the relationship between absence of evidence and nonbelief, then it is never rational to believe that anything doesn't exist—pixies, fairies, cheerful adolescents—unless you can prove for a fact they can't. Nearly a quarter of people have to bite this bullet.

Hit 10

Many claim that it is not justifiable to base one's beliefs about the external world on a firm, inner conviction, paying no regard to the external evidence, or lack of it, for the truth or falsity of this conviction. But if you do so, you cannot also say that the rapist Peter Sutcliffe was justified in basing his beliefs about God's will solely on precisely such a conviction. That's a straight bull's-eye for the intellectual sniper, who hits one in ten.

Hit 11

If you look at Hit 10, you might think that not many would fall for it. However, by choosing slightly differently, even more (nearly a quarter) get this hit instead. These people say that it is justifiable to base one's beliefs about the external world on a firm, inner conviction, regardless of the external evidence, or lack of it, for the truth or falsity of this conviction. But they do not accept that the rapist Peter Sutcliffe was justified in doing just that. The example of the rapist has exposed that, in practice, people do not in fact agree that any belief is justified just because one is convinced of its truth. So they need to revise their opinions here. The intellectual sniper has scored another bull's-eye!

Bullet 8

If you are consistent in applying the principle that it is justifi-able to base one's beliefs about the external world on a firm, inner conviction, regardless of the external evidence, or lack of it, for the truth or falsity of this conviction, then you have to accept that people might be justified in their belief that terrible things are right. Nearly one in ten are consistent in this way and so agree that the rapist is justified in believing that he carries out the will of God. But what if you also think that God defines what is good and what is evil? To be consistent, you must think the rapist is justified in believing that he acts morally when he acts on his inner conviction, since he sincerely believes he does God's will, and God's will is morally right. To say that the rapist is justified in believing he acts morally is not quite the same as to think he is justified to act, but how would you argue that the former (which is troubling enough) doesn't lead to the latter?

Bullet 9

This is similar to Bullet 8. It needs to be bitten if you are consistent in applying the principle that it is justifiable to base one's beliefs about the external world on a firm, inner conviction, regardless of the external evidence, or lack of it, for the truth or falsity of this conviction. That means having to accept that people might be justified in their belief that God could demand something terrible. This is something many religious people are willing to accept. For example, Kierkegaard believed that it is precisely because Abraham had to contravene established morality to follow God's will and attempt to sacrifice his son that his act was the supreme act of faith. But as Kierkegaard also stressed, this makes the act incomprehensible from a rational point of view. The rational alternative—that people should require more than such an inner conviction to justify such a belief—is more attractive to most people, but you reject this alternative and bite the bullet, along with around 8% of others.

Hit 12

If you agree that any being that it is right to call God must be free and have the power to do anything, you're set up for a hit, since we didn't put any limits on what "anything" is. Hence if you later say that God does not have the freedom and power to do impossible things such as create square circles, God is not free and does not have the power to do what is impossible. This requires that you accept—in common with most theologians, but contrary to your earlier answer—that God's freedom and power are not unbounded. She does not have the freedom and power to do *literally* anything. Some 10% of people took this hit, possibly feeling aggrieved. But we did warn you to read the statements carefully!

Bullet 10

This is the only hit or bullet you can take by agreeing to only one statement: God has the freedom and power to do that which is logically impossible (like creating square circles). If you say this, you are claiming that any discussion of God and ultimate reality cannot be constrained by basic principles of rationality. This would seem to make rational discourse about God impossible. If rational discourse about God is impossible, there is nothing rational we can say about God and nothing rational we can say to support our belief or disbelief in God. To reject rational constraints on religious discourse in this fashion requires accepting that religious convictions, including your religious convictions, are beyond any debate or rational discussion. This is to bite a bullet. Perhaps surprisingly, however, it's a bullet over 40% bite. This may be because people make a simple error: they think this means God could define circles and squares as she likes and thus make square circles. But this is not logically impossible, as the question specified. What is logically impossible is to make a square circle: a square has four sides and a circle one. We're not talking about God's power to rewrite the dictionary.

Hit 13

This is a flagrant contradiction. If you agree that it is justifiable to base one's beliefs about the external world on a firm, inner conviction, regardless of the external evidence, or lack of it, for the truth or falsity of this conviction, you cannot consistently say that it is not justifiable to believe in God on just these grounds. Still, around 4% suffer this hit.

Hit 14

This is an equally flagrant but opposite contradiction to Hit 13. If you agree that it is not justifiable to base one's beliefs about the external world on a firm, inner conviction, paying no regard to the external evidence, or lack of it, for the truth or falsity of this conviction, you cannot say it's justifiable to believe in God on just these grounds. Over one in five hold both beliefs, nonetheless.

Hit 15

It may be surprising that anyone takes this hit, but 5% do. They claim that it is not justifiable to believe in God based only on inner convictions and also that it was justifiable for the serial rapist to draw conclusions about God's will on the same grounds. If this form of justification is good enough for the rapist, why is it not good enough for the believer in God? There's an inconsistency here.

Hit 16

Under 3% of people agree that it is foolish to believe in God without certain, irrevocable proof that she exists, but also that it is justifiable to believe in God if one has a firm, inner conviction that God exists, regardless of the external evidence, or lack of it, for the truth or falsity of the conviction that God exists. However, a firm, inner conviction can never be certain proof, since many people have firm, inner convictions about things about which they are wrong (such as the guilt or innocence of suspects, for example). The second judgment is foolish, according to the first!

Final thoughts

Of all the tests in this book, Battleground God has been both the most popular and the most controversial. It seems that people do not like to have their views about God and religion challenged. Yet among intelligent and reflective believers, we have found Battleground God has been welcomed. Rabbi Julia Neuberger, for example, was enthusiastic when talking about it on the BBC World Service with Jeremy, and many philosophy teachers and professors have set it as a task for their students.

What is perhaps telling about this is that these advocates of Battleground God are precisely those people who are most keenly aware of its limitations. They know that the issues it raises run much deeper than yes or no answers to a set of simple questions. What they value, we suppose, is that it encourages rational reflection of issues of belief and exposes fairly basic intellectual difficulties that nevertheless often go unnoticed.

People who e-mail us to tell us we're anything from sad and

stupid to plain evil, however, don't seem to welcome rational scrutiny at all. We find this dispiriting. Why is it that those who are most keen to celebrate the unshakable fortitude of faith are so often the same people who think a beginners-level philosophy or religion activity is such a threat? Battleground God is a deep challenge only to those whose beliefs have shallow foundations. Which may just be many more of us than we like to think.

6

Taboo

To make our idea of morality center on forbidden acts is to defile the imagination and to introduce into our judgments of our fellow men a secret element of gusto.

Robert Louis Stevenson

Taboos are universal. In every society, there are forms of behavior considered so abhorrent that to participate in them is to risk vilification, ostracism and even death. The incest taboo, for example, is present in every human culture, and in the Western world incest almost everywhere is illegal. Perhaps you think that there are good reasons for the existence of such a taboo? For instance, children born as a result of incestuous relationships are more likely to suffer genetic problems than other children.

But not all taboos are like that. What about certain religious prohibitions, such as the Muslim one against eating pork? Do these have a rational grounding? It is certainly the case that most Muslims believe that eating pork is wrong. But is it possible to offer good reasons for such a belief? And what about prohibitions that most people in the West would accept as being inviolate, such as that it is wrong for children under the age of eighteen to have sexual relationships with adults? Are we committed to such taboos for good reasons that we can articulate, or is it just that we find certain kinds of behavior unacceptable for reasons to do with deep-rooted gut feelings?

Test your taboos

We're about to ask you for your responses to four taboo scenarios. You will need to treat the scenarios outlined *as if* they are descriptions of real-world events—and respond accordingly. In other words, what we're interested in here are your judgments about the events *precisely* as they are described in these scenarios, not as you think they would actually occur in the real world.

You will be asked to make Yes/No choices. If you aren't sure whether you're a "Yes" or a "No," please choose the response you are more inclined toward. Now you should be ready to give your responses. After each scenario you will be presented with a table containing two questions. Tick the box that contains your chosen answer to each one.

Scenario 1

An old woman was very ill. On her deathbed she asked her son to promise that he would visit her grave at least once a week. The son didn't want to disappoint his mother, so he promised that he would. But after his mother died, he didn't keep his promise. He was too busy. He didn't tell anyone about his promise, and he has never felt guilty for failing to do as he said he would.

A How do you judge the failure of the son to visit his mother's grave once a week as he promised?	He was wrong	He was not wrong

B Suppose you learn about two foreign countries. In one country, it is normal for a son to break a deathbed promise to his mother to visit her grave every week. In the other, if a son has made such a promise, then it is normal for him to keep his word. Are both these customs OK morally speaking or is one of them bad or morally wrong?	Both customs are OK	One custom is bad

Scenario 2

A family's cat was killed by a car in front of their home. They had heard that cat meat was very tasty, so they cut up the cat, cooked it and ate it for dinner. To date, they have never regretted the decision and they have not suffered any harm as a result of cooking and eating the cat.

A How do you judge the actions of the family in eating their pet cat?	They were wrong	They were not wrong
B Suppose you learn about two foreign countries. In one country, it is normal to eat the family pet if it is killed in a road accident. In the other, pets killed in road accidents are not normally eaten. Are both these customs OK morally speaking or is one of them bad or morally wrong?	Both customs are OK	One custom is bad

Scenario 3

Sarah and Peter are brother and sister. They were on holiday together away from home. One night they were staying alone in a tent on a beach. They decided it would be fun to have sex. They were both over 21. They had sex and enjoyed it. They knew that for medical reasons Sarah could not get pregnant. They decided not to have sex with each other again, but they never regretted having had sex once. In fact, it remained a positive experience for them throughout their lives. It also remained entirely their secret (until now!).

A	How do you judge Sarah and Peter's actions?	They were wrong	They were not wrong
B	Suppose you learn about two foreign countries. In one country, it is normal for brothers and sisters to have sex with each other on one occasion if the sister is infertile. In the other, brothers and sisters never have sex with each other. Are both these customs OK morally speaking or is one of them bad and morally wrong?	Both customs are OK	One custom is bad

Scenario 4

A man goes to his local grocery store once a week and buys a frozen chicken. But before cooking and eating the chicken, he has sexual intercourse with it. Then he cooks it and eats it. He never tells anyone about what he does, never regrets it and never shows any ill effects from behaving this way. He remains an upstanding member of his community.

A	How do you judge this man's actions (assume there are no ethical problems with meat eating!)?	They were wrong	They were not wrong
B	Suppose you learn about two foreign countries. In one country, it is normal for people to have secret sex with dead chickens. In the other, people don't in the normal course of events have intercourse with frozen poultry. Are both these customs OK morally speaking or is one of them bad and morally wrong?	Both customs are OK	One custom is bad

Scoring

The scoring here is not complicated, but it does require several steps, so follow each one carefully.

1 For each scenario, if you answered "wrong" to the first question (A), you should tick the box for that scenario under A (see grid below). And if you responded that "one custom is bad" to the second question (B), you should put a tick in the box under B.

	A = wrong	B = one custom is bad
Scenario 1		
Scenario 2		
Scenario 3		
Scenario 4		
Totals		

2 Calculate the total for column A by simply adding up the number of ticks in column A.

3 Calculate the total for column B by only adding up the number of ticks in column B that are matched by a tick in column A for the same scenario. So if there is a tick in column B but not in column A for a scenario, you don't count it for the total.

You now need to convert these totals into two quotient scores.

4   The total in column A is your *Moralizing Quotient*. Make a note of it in the grid below.

5   If the total in column B is 0, and your total in column A is 1 or more, then your *Universalizing Factor* is 0, and you can enter that into the grid below.

6   If the total in column A is 0, then your *Universalizing Factor* is −1, regardless of what your total is in column B.

7   If neither 5 nor 6 applies and you haven't yet got your *Universalizing Factor*, then you need to do a bit of math. All you have to do is divide the total in column B by the total in column A. This is your *Universalizing Factor*, and you can enter that into the grid below.

	Your scores
Moralizing Quotient	
Universalizing Factor	

What your scores mean

Your *Moralizing Quotient* is a measure of your tendency to condemn the actions described in these scenarios as morally wrong. A score of 4 indicates a *fully moralizing* position, one that judges each of the actions in the four scenarios as being wrong. A score of 0 is a *fully permissive* response, one that judges none of the actions in the four scenarios as being wrong. So the closer your score is to 4, the more your position is moralizing, and the closer to 0, the more it is permissive.

The average moralizing quotient among the tens of thousands who have done this activity on the *The Philosophers' Magazine* Web site is about 1.5.

Your *Universalizing Factor* is a measure of your tendency to judge moral wrongdoing in universal terms. A score of 1 indicates a *fully universalizing* position, one that says acts that are wrong are so regardless of prevailing cultural norms and social conventions. A score of 0, on the other hand, indicates a *fully relativizing* position, one that says whether an act is to be thought of as wrong is largely a matter of social norms, and that it is quite possible that what is wrong in one culture may not be wrong in another. A score of –1 means that you saw no moral wrong in any of the activities depicted in these scenarios, and so it is not possible to determine the extent to which you see moral wrongdoing in universal terms.

Together, your scores tell you whether you are more moralizing than permissive, and if not fully permissive, whether you are more universalizing than relativizing.

Analysis

So what's the payoff here? Why are we interested in the nature of these kinds of moral judgments?

Most of us would probably like to believe we are able to give good reasons for the moral judgments that we make. For example, if we were asked why it is wrong for an older girl to push a younger boy off a swing, we might talk about the fact that the boy's rights had been violated or about the fact that he experienced some physical harm. While it is true that the philosophical waters would soon become muddied if we examined our reasoning more carefully, we are able to give at least superficially good reasons for our judgment of moral wrongdoing.

However, there is a class of activities in which it is much more difficult to offer arguments to support a judgment of moral wrong. This is the class of activities that are harmless (at least in a narrow sense), private and consensual yet violate strong social norms. The examples we used in this activity had to do with the taboos and rituals associated with death, food and sexuality.

No doubt some people will suspect that we have constructed this activity with the intention of showing that people are just mistaken if they think that things like having sex with a frozen chicken are wrong. This is not the case, since it *is* possible to at least *make arguments* that such things are wrong. For example, you might argue that human beings are God's creations, and their sexuality is a gift from God to be enjoyed only in the context of a monogamous union between one man and one woman. Chickens, frozen or otherwise, are not part of the picture. Therefore, to have sex with one is to abuse the gift of sexuality and will necessarily harm a person's relationship with God. It follows that having sex with poultry is a moral wrong.

Our intention is not to show that the moral prohibitions surrounding taboos cannot be justified, but that there are tensions in the way that people reason about morality. One important tension has to do with how central the idea of harm is to many moral frameworks. Previous research suggests that, with the exception of the siblings story, most people judge the scenarios presented here to involve harm neither to the protagonists nor to anybody else; but that, regardless, plenty of people still think that these scenarios depict acts that are morally wrong.

The key question here is: can an action be morally wrong if it is entirely private and no one, not even the person doing/ engaged in the act, is harmed by it at all? Presented starkly, many people are inclined to answer no. Yet the same people often judge some of the actions in Taboo to be wrong, even though there is no harm caused to anyone. This looks like a straight contradiction. Is there any way out of it?

It could be argued that, contrary to appearances, there is harm in the acts depicted here. These scenarios have been set up precisely in such a way that it seems that no harm has occurred, the protagonists suffer no ill effects as a result of their actions and their actions remain private. But perhaps you cannot accept these stipulations: the belief that some harm, at least to one's moral integrity, would be caused by these actions makes pretending that it wouldn't psychologically impossible.

But it is possible that such a belief that harm occurs is a rationalization after the event of a prior intuition that the acts depicted here are morally wrong. In other words, people don't like things like incest and sex with poultry, and they are pretty good at inventing stories to explain why they don't like them, but, in fact, these "explanations" don't really explain anything at all. The negative reaction is more visceral. We already know that people engage in this kind of retroactive reasoning when justifying their responses to taboo-type stimuli. We also know that judgments of wrongdoing by people who take a moralizing stance toward the kinds of acts depicted here are better predicted by asking them whether they would be bothered to see these acts than by asking them whether anyone is harmed. The suspicion, then, is that a judgment that harm occurs is often simply a buttress of a prior baseline moral commitment.

Some are just happy to argue that an action can be wrong even if it is entirely private and nobody, not even the person doing the act, is harmed by it. But there are still difficulties with this kind of argument. For example, while it is easy enough to claim that siblings should not have sex with one another because it violates the rules governing human sexuality that have been laid down by God, it is much more difficult to show *what* is wrong with violating these rules, unless one talks about harm (though, of course, there is nothing to stop one simply asserting that it is wrong to break rules). Thus one finds the idea in Christian theology that man is harmed by his sins in that they constitute a barrier between himself and God.

Some philosophers have gone so far as to suggest that a notion of "harm," understood in a certain kind of way, is a prerequisite of proper moral reasoning. For example, Jeremy Bentham, the founder of classical utilitarianism, argued that pleasure and pain (a "positive harm") are the only proper measures of value. In his terms, then, a wrong act is one that increases pain (or that, given equally possible choices, results in the least pleasure). Although utilitarianism has moved on since Bentham's day, it is still possible to find philosophers who are willing to argue that the central concern of moral philosophy is the consequences of actions, where only those with bad ones can be considered wrong.

The "yuck factor"

One of the interesting things that previous research has found when exploring people's reactions to the scenarios featured in this activity is that people who have very strong emotional responses to these stories frequently find it difficult to provide an explanation or justification for what they are feeling. According to Steve Pinker, this is because our moral convictions are rooted not so much in reason as in the evolutionary makeup of our minds. In his words: "People have gut feelings that give them emphatic moral convictions, and they struggle to rationalize them after the fact. These convictions may have little to do with moral judgments that one could justify to others in terms of their effects on happiness or suffering. They arise instead from the neurobiological and evolutionary design of the organs we call moral emotions" (*The Blank Slate*).

The dangers of rooting moral attitudes in emotion are obvious. It means that a "yuck factor" might lead us to condemn actions—and even people—we have no good reason to condemn. For example, consider the fate of the untouchables in the Indian caste system. Although much discrimination against them is technically outlawed, in practice many are not allowed to touch people from the higher castes; they are not allowed to drink from the same wells; on public occasions, they have to sit at a distance from everybody else. In some regions, even contact with the shadow of an untouchable person is seen as polluting and necessitates a purification ritual. Such prohibitions might sit easily with a certain kind of raw sentiment. They are much harder, if not impossible, to justify in the light of reason.

However, one must be careful not simply to assume that emotion has no role to play in moral reasoning. Indeed, some philosophers claim that it is a mistake to think that moral judgment involves anything other than emotion. A. J. Ayer, for example, argued that ethical statements are *nothing more* than the expression of emotional attitudes. He denied that it was possible for ethical statements to be factually true. "Murder is wrong" is not a statement that is true or false but functions more as an exclamation like "murder—*booo!*"

Even if one does not accept this kind of extreme "emotivism," it is still fairly easy to see that emotion can play some kind of role in good moral reasoning. Empathy, for example, would seem to be an important component of a proper moral outlook. It is hard to imagine that the atrocities of the Holocaust would have occurred had its protagonists been more able to imagine themselves in the emotional position of their victims. Indeed, the philosopher Jonathan Glover has argued that many of the atrocities of the last century were possible precisely because people's moral emotions had been switched off.

Nevertheless, it is probably right that we are suspicious of moral judgments that are rooted solely in the "yuck factor." Steve Pinker, in *The Blank Slate*, puts it like this: "The difference between a defensible moral position and an atavistic gut feeling is that with the former we can give *reasons* why our conviction is valid."

Final thoughts

One difficulty with encouraging philosophical self-examination is that many people miss the point of it. You question the reasons for believing God exists and they assume you are trying to convince them he doesn't. You question our capacity for rational thought and they assume you are trying to say they are stupid. You question the rational basis for taboos and they assume you're trying to overthrow them all and campaign for a nation in which incest, pedophilia and desecrating graves are the norm.

It would be pointless to think the unthinkable if you never allowed for the possibility that the unthinkable might sometimes be true. So you do need to be open to the possibility that we would be better off without at least some of our taboos. Skepticism about social norms is an empty pose if it doesn't threaten any of them. But the real point is to open up our thinking, to countenance the repulsive because, if we don't, our prejudices will get in the way of finding proper justifications.

Wittgenstein once said that philosophy leaves the world as it is. As usual, it's not entirely obvious what he meant by that. But what he seemed to be suggesting was that the main purpose of probing our ideas and values ever deeper is not to change them but to understand them.

7

Morality Play

Heaven and hell suppose two distinct species of men, the good and the bad; but the greatest part of mankind float betwixt vice and virtue.

David Hume

Whatever its flaws, Roman Catholicism got one thing absolutely right: the thought that we are being morally judged tends to make us deeply uncomfortable, guilty and even scared. By making confession of sins such a central part of its practice, the Catholic Church has managed to keep a strong emotional grip on its members.

But you needn't worry about being judged here—for once. Morality Play is not a test of your moral fiber. Rather, it reveals something about the framework of your moral thinking, something that is not generally given as much attention as perhaps it should be. What's even better, no matter what your framework turns out to be, we have no way of saying whether you have done well or badly. So, proceed and fear not that thou shalt be judged . . .

Find your framework

We're going to present you with nineteen different scenarios. In each case, you must make a judgment about what is the morally right thing to do. It is important to remember that at no time are your responses going to be judged "correct" or "incorrect."

You should respond with what you think is the morally right thing to do (which may not be the same as what you would actually do).

Several questions talk about "moral obligation." In this activity, to say you are morally obliged to do something means that, in order to behave morally, you must do that thing. When the moral obligation is "strong," this means not doing what is obligated of you is a serious wrongdoing; when the obligation is "weak," failing to do what is obligated of you is still a wrongdoing, but not a serious one. Conventional morality, for example, would say we have a strong obligation not to torture innocent people and a weak obligation to say thank you for minor favors.

Finally, remember to read each scenario very carefully. You will find that there are similarities between some of the scenarios. However, don't let this lure you into responding without thinking—each scenario needs some thought!

Questions

1 You pass someone in the street who is in severe need and you are able to help at little cost to yourself. Are you morally obliged to do so?

    a. Strongly obliged
    b. Weakly obliged
    c. Not obliged

2 You have a brother. You know that someone has been seriously injured as a result of criminal activity undertaken by him. You live in a country where the police are generally trust-worthy. Are you morally obliged to inform them about your brother's crime?

a. Strongly obliged
b. Weakly obliged
c. Not obliged

3 Do you think that assisting the suicide of someone who wants to die—and has requested help—is morally equivalent to allowing them to die by withholding medical assistance (assuming that the level of suffering turns out to be identical in both cases)?

a. Yes
b. No

4 You are able to help some people. Unfortunately, you can only do so by harming other people. The number of people harmed will always be 10% of those helped. When considering whether it is morally justified to help, does the actual number of people involved make any difference? For example, does it make a difference if you are helping ten people by harming one person rather than helping 100,000 people by harming 10,000 people?

a. Yes
b. No

5 You own an unoccupied property. You are contacted by a refugee group that desperately needs somewhere to house a person seeking asylum who is being unjustly persecuted in a foreign country. Your anonymity is assured. You have every reason to believe that no harm will come to your property. Are you morally obliged to allow them to use your property?

a. Strongly obliged
b. Weakly obliged
c. Not obliged

6 A charity collection takes place in your office. For every $10 given, a blind person's sight is restored. Instead of donating $10, you use the money to treat yourself to a cocktail after work. Are you morally responsible for the continued blindness of the person who would have been treated had you made the donation?

a. Responsible
b. Partly responsible
c. Not responsible

7 Someone you have never met needs a kidney transplant. You are one of the few people who can provide the kidney. Would any moral obligation to provide the kidney be greater if this person were a cousin rather than a stranger?

a. Yes
b. No

8 You can save the lives of one thousand patients by cancelling one hundred operations that would have saved the lives of one hundred different patients. Are you morally obliged to do so?

a. Yes
b. No

9 Are your moral obligations to people in your own country or community stronger than those to people in other countries and communities (assuming no unusual circumstances—e.g., suffering because of famine—in either your own country/community or other countries/communities)?

a. Yes
b. No

10 You deliberately sabotage a piece of machinery in your workplace so that when someone next uses it there will be an accident that results in that person losing the use of their legs. Are you morally responsible for their injury?

a. Responsible
b. Partly responsible
c. Not responsible

11 You know the identity of someone who has committed a serious crime resulting in a person being badly injured. Are you morally obliged to reveal their identity to an appropriate authority so that they are dealt with justly?

a. Strongly obliged
b. Weakly obliged
c. Not obliged

12 You can save the lives of ten innocent people by killing one other innocent person. Are you morally obliged to do so?

a. Yes
b. No

13 You see an advertisement from a charity in a newspaper about a person in severe need on the other side of the world. You can help this person at little cost to yourself. Are you morally obliged to do so?

   a. Strongly obliged
   b. Weakly obliged
   c. Not obliged

14 You are required to send a person a gift and you have bought a bottle of drink to send to them. However, you discover it is poison and if consumed will cause blindness in the drinker. To replace it with a noncontaminated bottle will cost you $10. You give the poisoned drink as a gift anyway. Are you morally responsible for the blindness of the drinker?

   a. Responsible
   b. Partly responsible
   c. Not responsible

15 A situation arises in which you can either save your own child from death or contact the emergency services in order to save the lives of ten other children. You cannot do both, and there is no way to save everyone. Which course of action are you morally obliged to follow?

   a. Save your own child
   b. Save ten other children

16 You can save the lives of ten patients by cancelling one operation that would have saved the life of a different patient. Are you morally obliged to do so?

a. Yes
b. No

17 You own an unoccupied property. You are contacted by a welfare organization that desperately needs somewhere to house a person from a nearby town who is being unjustly persecuted. Your anonymity is assured. You have every reason to believe that no harm will come to your property. Are you morally obliged to allow them to use your property?

a. Strongly obliged
b. Weakly obliged
c. Not obliged

18 You become aware that a piece of machinery in your workplace is faulty and that if it is not repaired there will soon be an accident that will result in someone losing the use of their legs. Despite knowing that nobody else is aware of the fault, you take no action. Shortly afterward, the accident occurs and someone does lose the use of their legs. Are you morally responsible for their injury?

a. Responsible
b. Partly responsible
c. Not responsible

19 You can save the lives of one million innocent people by killing one hundred thousand others. Are you morally obliged to do so?

a. Yes
b. No

How to score

The scoring here may look complicated, but it really isn't. Just follow each step carefully. To analyze your responses, you need to score your answers, putting the results in the grid opposite. Once again, be reassured that, since there is no right or wrong, higher scores are not better than lower ones.

1 For those question numbers paired (e.g., 1 & 13), you score by seeing how similar they are.

- If you answered the same for both questions, no matter what answer you chose, then score 10.
- If you answered differently where there were three choices, score 0 if your answers were nonadjacent letters (a and c or vice versa) and 5 if they were adjacent letters (a and b, or b and c).
- In questions in which only two choices of answers were available, score 0 if they were different.

2 For the questions that are by themselves in the boxes, score the following:

Q. 3   a = 10, b = 0

Qs. 4, 7, 9 & 15   a = 0, b = 10

3 Add up your four totals for each of the boxes GD, AO, FR and SC in turn.

4 Add these four numbers together for your grand total.

GD	Score
Qs.1 & 13	
Q. 9	
Qs. 17 & 5	
Total GD	

AO	Score
Qs. 14 & 6	
Q. 3	
Qs. 18 & 10	
Total AO	

FR	Score
Q. 15	
Qs. 2 & 11	
Q. 7	
Total FR	

SC	Score
Qs. 12 & 19	
Qs. 16 & 8	
Q. 4	
Total SC	

Grand total	

What's your moral framework?

The higher your score, the more parsimonious your moral framework. So what does that mean? It's a phrase we've coined ourselves, but the general idea is not a new one.

Moral frameworks can be more or less parsimonious. That is to say, they can employ a wide range of principles that vary in their application according to circumstances (less parsimonious), or they can employ a small range of principles that apply across a wide range of circumstances without modification (more parsimonious).

An example might make this clearer. If we assume that we are committed to the principle that it is a good to reduce suffering, the test of moral parsimony is to see whether this principle is applied simply and without modification or qualification in a number of different circumstances. Supposing, for example, we find that in otherwise identical circumstances, the principle is applied differently if the suffering person is from a different country from our own. This suggests a lack of moral parsimony, because the rule "reduce suffering" is qualified by other rules to do with proximity. The idea of moral parsimony should become even clearer as we go through the more detailed analysis.

The higher your score, the more parsimonious your moral framework. In other words, a high score is suggestive of a moral framework that comprises a minimal number of moral principles that apply across a range of circumstances and acts without qualification or exception. We suggest that any total score above 90 (out of 120) should be considered indicative of a parsimonious moral framework. Any score of 60 or less suggests a particularly unparsimonious framework. In practice, the average score for online players of the game is 78, which is not especially parsimonious.

We make no judgment about whether moral parsimony is a good or bad thing. Some people will think that on balance it is a good thing and that we should strive to minimize the number of moral principles that form our moral frameworks. On this view, moral parsimony can be seen as indicative of moral consistency, something that is usually considered a virtue.

Others will suspect that moral parsimony is likely to render moral frameworks simplistic and that an overly parsimonious moral framework will leave us unable to deal with the complexity of real circumstances and acts. The accusation against the morally parsimonious person is of excessive rigidity, or moral autism.

However, there is more to this test than revealing your overall degree of moral parsimony. There are some more interesting subdivisions.

Delving deeper

If you are less than entirely parsimonious, then what factors lead you to vary your moral rules? The questions in this activity were designed to factor in the effects of four kinds of differences that may affect moral judgment.

Geographical Distance (GD)

This category has to do with the impact of geographical distance on the application of moral principles. The idea here is to determine whether moral principles are applied equally when dealing with sets of circumstances and acts that differ *only* in their geographical location in relation to the person making the judgment.

Although we promised not to judge you, to be honest it should be admitted that most moral theories claim that geographical difference should not be a morally relevant factor. However, it's not quite as simple as this, since many would say that we are more obligated toward members of our own communities than we are to others, so, in fact, geographical distance may be taken as a proxy for community difference.

Online, with an average score of 26.4 out of 30, this category manifested the equal highest average level of parsimony. How do you compare?

We also tried a little trick online. Most of our Web site visitors are from North America and Great Britain. So we varied one question so that half the people were asked if they were obliged to help people in India, and the other half people in Australia. The point here was that most respondents would be white and of Anglo-Saxon origin, like the Australians, not the Indians. Would that make a difference? Hearteningly, it seems not. There was just a 1% difference, with slightly more feeling obligated to help Australians than Indians. Given the large number of respondents, this is still statistically significant—that is to say, it probably measures a real difference and falls outside the margin of error. But 1% is such a small number, it at least suggests that the vast majority are able to keep considerations of skin color out of their moral deliberations.

Family Relatedness (FR)

In this category, we look at the impact of family loyalty and ties on the way in which moral principles are applied. The idea here is to determine whether moral principles are applied without modification or qualification when you're dealing with sets of circumstances and acts that differ only in whether the participants are related through family ties to the person making the judgment.

Not surprisingly, this was the least parsimonious of the categories. The average parsimony score was just 19.5 out of 30.

Acts and Omissions (AO)

This category has to do with whether there is a difference between the moral status of acting and omitting to act where the consequences are the same in both instances. Consider the following example: Assume that on the whole it is a bad thing if a person is poisoned while drinking a cola drink. One might then ask whether there is a moral difference between poisoning the cola, on the one hand (an act), and failing to prevent a person from drinking a cola someone else has poisoned, when in a position to do so, on the other (an omission). In this category, then, the idea is to determine if moral principles are applied equally when you're dealing with sets of circumstances that differ only in whether the participants have acted or omitted to act.

This was another category with a low parsimony score: 21.6. This suggests people tend to think it does make a significant difference whether something is the result of an act or an omission. This is one of the biggest debates in moral philosophy and is also critical to laws concerning euthanasia. For many, a line is crossed when physicians move from allowing someone to die, even if they can stop that happening, and actually killing them.

Scale (SC)

This final category has to do with whether scale is a factor in making moral judgments. A simple example will make this clear. Consider a situation in which it is possible to save ten lives by sacrificing one life. Is there a moral difference between this choice and one in which the numbers of lives involved are different but proportional—for example, saving one hundred lives by sacrificing ten? In this category, then, the idea is to determine whether moral principles are applied without modification or qualification when you're dealing with sets of circumstances that differ only in their scale, as in the sense described above.

The reason we thought this might make a difference is that large-scale suffering has more of an emotional impact on us. Whenever there is a rail crash, for example, in which a number of people die, it captures the news headlines, even though as many people or more died on the roads over the same period of the reporting.

The average parsimony score of 26.4 in this category was the same as for geographical distance. It seems people do think scale makes some difference, but not a very significant one.

Final thoughts

The reason why we cannot say whether your responses are right or wrong is that Morality Play deals with one of the toughest sets of issues in moral theory. On the one hand, we can't just go around making ad hoc adjustments to moral principles to suit ourselves. On the other, we cannot fail to take into account the differing circumstances in which moral judgments come into play.

This activity invites you to consider seriously whether the distinctions you make are justified or self-serving. For instance, even if it is morally justifiable to consider your family more than strangers, does this have limits? What if you use your influence to get your child into a school when another deserves the place even more? And even if it is justifiable to prioritize our own communities, when does this turn into a prejudiced or callous disregard for members of others? Morality Play is just a game, but these moral choices are not.

8

Shakespeare vs. Britney Spears

A painting in a museum hears more ridiculous opinions than anything else in the world.

Edmond de Goncourt

What makes something a great work of art? Which artists have produced the world's greatest art? These questions provoke endless and probably inconclusive arguments. Yet we can't stop asking them. Perhaps it is because, although the answers are never final, we cannot accept that there are no answers at all. If someone claims that the works of REO Speedwagon are much better than those of Mozart, or that Ozzy Osbourne is a greater poet than Keats, most of us don't just feel we have different tastes— we feel that in some sense the other person is plainly wrong.

This test explores what you really think makes a great work of art. Who knows, maybe according to your criteria REO Speedwagon *are* musical geniuses after all.

Preparation: What is great art?

There are endless answers to the question of what makes a great work of art, but six broad types of answer have been given time and again in the history of art theory and aesthetics. What you will need to do is to say how important you think each factor is in assessing whether something is a good work of art.

To help you decide, we've included brief descriptions of what philosophers have said about each factor. You should read these first so you can be sure we all mean the same thing. Once you've done that, move on to Part One.

Aesthetic criteria

The work displays great technical ability

Interestingly, the issue of an artist's skill has not been a central one in the history of philosophical aesthetics and does not normally constitute the core of any philosopher's conception of art. Sometimes it is taken for granted that skill is required, since what was considered art always required technical skill for its creation. But since the advent of conceptual art and the possibility that an object, such as a urinal, could become a work of art merely by being conceptualized in a certain way, the role of the artist's skill in art has become a more salient issue.

There have also been philosophers who have argued that there is no place for the artist in the appreciation of the work of art, which implies that one need not consider whether the artist was skilled. One manifestation of this is the idea of the intentional fallacy, put forward by Wimslatt and Beardsley. "The design or intention of the author," they wrote, "is neither available nor desirable as a standard for judging the success of a work of literary art." What they say about the author could equally be said of other artists.

In contrast, the contemporary British philosopher Roger Scruton has written that "A person for whom it makes no difference whether a sculpture was carved by wind and rain or by human hand would be a person incapable of interpreting, indeed incapable of perceiving, sculptures." For Scruton, it is vital to aesthetic appreciation at least to see the artwork as something that has been created by design by an artist.

The work is enjoyable

Many philosophers have considered the pleasure that art gives us as vital to its value. But virtually all who do so insist on making some distinction between "proper," aesthetic pleasure and other pleasures that we may feel.

This distinction is made very clear by Kant. He argued that true aesthetic pleasure is "disinterested." What Kant means by this is that the pleasure must be independent of any consideration of whether the object of aesthetic appreciation actually exists. Consider, for example, the pleasure we take in looking at an attractive man or woman. Much of this pleasure is not disinterested, in Kant's sense, because it is linked with a desire for that person. The possibility—real or imagined—of enjoying this person in the flesh is part of the pleasure we take in looking at them. For there to be genuine aesthetic appreciation of a person, that pleasure must be purely in the contemplation of their appearance, regardless of any thought as to their real existence.

Many other philosophers have tried to distinguish between pure aesthetic pleasure and other, cruder pleasures. Coomaraswamy, for instance, talks about the Indian concept of *rasa*, which is a distinctive form of aesthetic pleasure, to be distinguished from ordinary pleasures such as eating and drinking. The experience of *rasa* is more akin to religious experience than sensory enjoyment.

Of course, this means that if millions of people enjoy the music of Britney Spears, it is possible to argue that this is not proper aesthetic pleasure. Whether this distinction is justifiable or merely an excuse for snobbery is a question for another time.

The work conveys the feelings of the artist

The idea that art is essentially about communicating the feelings of the artist is a romantic one that has wide, popular appeal. R. G. Collingwood concurs with the basis of this characterization of art. However, one should be careful not to misunderstand what this means for him. It does not mean that art is a kind of spontaneous outburst of emotion. On the contrary, the skill of the artist lies in their ability to articulate their emotions through their chosen art form. Art expresses the artist's feelings and conveys them to its audience, but it is not a mere expression of feelings, like a whoop, a scream or a cry.

Tolstoy held a similar view. He thought the object of a work of art is to induce feelings in the viewer, reader or listener. Again, on this view, the artist is doing much more than merely expressing how they feel—they have to have the skill and ability to induce this same feeling in their audience. The other important thing to note about Tolstoy is that he believes that unless the emotion being induced is morally uplifting in some way, the work of art has no value. Not for him the romantic idea that the artist must express how they feel, whatever it is; the artist should only convey higher emotions.

The work conveys an important moral lesson or helps us to live better lives

The idea that art must be morally uplifting in some way may seem a quaint one today, when art is often considered to be, if anything, exempt from the ordinary standards of ethics. There is a romantic view of the artist as someone who should not be censored but be given the freedom to express themselves and create as their muse takes them.

However, there is a tradition of arguing for the importance

of morality in art. Tolstoy appealed to morality because he thought it obvious that whether or not we enjoy a work of art or appreciate it in any other way is an entirely subjective matter. Any attempts to prescribe standards of taste objectively are doomed to failure. However, there was one way in which we could judge art objectively, and that is on its moral content. So, for example, when judging whether a novel is a good or bad read, we are just expressing our opinions. But when we ask whether the novel conveys a morally virtuous message, we can come to a conclusion that all sensible judges can agree upon.

This argument is important because it has consequences for the public subsidy of art. Tolstoy thought that it was unjustifiable to subsidize the arts if their value was in the enjoyment they gave. Why subsidize some pleasures such as opera and dance, while at the same time taxing others, such as drink and entertainments?

Others have argued for the moral importance of art on other grounds. Schiller argued that through art we are able to open ourselves up to the world and yet make sense of it to ourselves through the creative play art offers. This enables us to cultivate ourselves in ways that make us better people.

The formal features of the work are harmonious and/or beautiful

Works of art are often seen as representational: a portrait represents a person, a novel represents a series of events and a piece of music, perhaps, represents an emotion. However, there have also been many people who have argued against this conception of art. An alternative view is that it is not the fact that art represents (if indeed anything is represented) that makes great art. Rather, it is the way in which the formal features of the work of art come together.

This is most evident if you consider a cubist or abstract

painting. What makes such a work of art great is the way in which the colors, shapes and textures come together to form a harmonious or pleasing whole. This is perhaps even more plausible in music, in which there is no obvious representing going on at all, but the sounds of the different instruments and their arrangement form a pleasing whole.

This idea was developed by Clive Bell in the early part of the twentieth century in his concept of a work of art's "significant form." The idea also appears in Kant, who thought proper aesthetic appreciation came only in the disinterested contemplation of artworks, in which considerations of what the art represents or relates to fall away and one considers the work merely in itself.

The major problem with this view of art is that it seems it cannot apply to all art. The power of Picasso's *Guernica*, for example, can only be explained if one says something about what it represents—the great suffering and torment of people and animals bombed by Franco in the Spanish Civil War. To consider only the formal aspects of that painting seems to miss out on what is vital to it.

The work reveals an insight into reality

Plato actually opposed art on the grounds that it was an obstacle to the proper understanding of reality. In his view, true reality is the realm of the "forms." The forms are the perfect "blueprints" of which actual objects are mere replicas. So, any particular chair, for example, is an inferior copy of the eternal form of the chair. Because art represents actual chairs and other objects, it is thus two steps removed from reality. Art is effectively a representation of copies of reality. Anyone who wants to understand reality is therefore advised to avoid art!

Fortunately, Plato is not the last word on this subject.

Opponents of Plato do not always explicitly state that art reveals the true reality behind appearances. However, they do often imply that art has an ability to help us understand reality better by revealing important, general features about it. Aristotle, for example, talked about tragedy as catharsis, which sees art as enabling us to deal with universal emotions by confronting them and, in a sense, purging them, through watching a drama. Hsun Tzu thought that music somehow reflects the harmony of the divine order, and so by cultivating a proper appreciation of music, we gain some insight into ultimate reality. Schopenhauer believed that art is an insight into the fundamental feature of reality: the will, which is the power behind all activity in the universe. And Dewey argued that art allows us to experience the unity of reality that is lost in the discord of everyday experience.

Take the test: Part One

Now it's time to find out what you think, and whether you think what you think you think.

Under "How important?", give each factor a score according to how important you think it is for making a work of art great. For the moment, ignore columns A–D.

The scores are:

Vital	4
Very important	3
Quite important	2
A little important	1
Not important at all	0

	How important?	A	B	C	D
Technical ability					
Enjoyability					
Expresses artist's feelings					
Moral or life lessons					
Harmony and beauty					
Insight into reality					

Once you've done that, you can move on to Part Two.

Part Two: From theory to practice

1 Think of two artists of any kind: writers, painters, composers, recording artists—it's your choice. You should be sufficiently familiar with the work of the artists that you choose so that you can answer a few general questions about it.

2 Decide which of the two you prefer. If you find that a hard choice, then imagine you are forced to choose between which person's works to take to a desert island. To avoid irrelevant factors, suppose that you can only take equivalent amounts of each artist's works, so, for example, don't choose Shakespeare over Sylvia Plath on the basis you'll have more if you choose the Bard. And please don't say you just can't choose.

3 Next, write the name of each artist in the grid on the previous page: one in the box beneath A and the other in the box beneath C.

4 Rate their works in terms of the factors in the first column, according to how far they generally reflect each factor, using this scoring system.

To the very highest degree 4

To a great degree 3

To a significant degree 2

To some degree 1

Not at all 0

For example, if you chose Weird Al Yankovic, and you think he is supremely enjoyable but offers no moral or life lessons, put 4 on the "Enjoyability" row and 0 on the "Moral or life lessons" row.

5 Now you need to do a bit of arithmetic. On each row you need to multiply the score in the "How important?" column and the score in column A, putting the result in column B. Then do the same with the score in the "How important?" column and the score in column C, putting that result in column D.

6 You then add up the scores in columns B and D—separately, of course.

Here's an example:

	How important?	**A** **Weird Al** **Yankovic**	**B**	**C** **Jeff** **Koons**	**D**
Technical ability	2	3	6	1	2
Enjoyability	3	4	12	1	3
Expresses artist's feelings	4	2	8	2	8
Moral or life lessons	0	0	0	2	0
Harmony and beauty	1	0	0	1	1
Insight into reality	3	0	0	3	9
			26		23

7 Now read on to find out what this all means.

Analysis

The scoring system is designed to show roughly how each artist rates according to your own criteria of what a great artist is. So, for example, an artist scores maximum points (4 x 4 = 16) if their works exhibit a vital factor to the highest degree. They score only 1 point (1 x 1), however, if their works contain only a little of what is in any case not a very important factor.

So, according to the criteria you have selected and the marks you have awarded each artist, the artist with the higher score is the greater artist. (In our example, Weird Al Yankovic beat Jeff Koons. Who did that scoring?)

Is your winner the same artist whose works you chose to take to a desert island? Probably. But if you were to repeat this exercise for a variety of artists (try it), you would probably find that on several occasions this is not what happens. It would, of course, be very tempting to put this down to quirks in our scoring system. But we think it can mean something else, namely that what people say they think makes a great work of art often doesn't correspond to what they actually value about the works of art they really love.

We have some evidence for this from data collected from online players of the games. Each had to give scores for two artists from a preselected list. Before showing what these scores meant, we asked them which of the two's works they would prefer to take to their desert island. What we found was that often people chose the artists who received the lower score according to their own criteria and judgments!

There are three explanations for why this happens. One is that our activity is flawed. Well, it certainly isn't perfect, but while this may explain some apparent anomalies, we don't think it accounts for the vast majority.

The second is that for many people, one aspect of art trumps all others, and usually that is its enjoyability. They may sincerely believe that, all things considered, Shakespeare is a greater artist than Britney Spears, but if they had to choose, they would rather dance on the beach to "Hit Me Baby One More Time" than watch *The Tempest*. If this is the case, then look back at the scores and you'll probably see that the artist ranked higher for enjoyment was the one taken to the desert island.

This is probably true a lot of the time. However, people—especially educated middle-class people, or those who want to appear cultivated—don't like to admit that, actually, great works of art don't do it for them like pop music, pop novels or Hollywood blockbusters.

That leads to the third explanation of the anomalies. People carry around with them an idea of what great art *should* be like. This doesn't necessarily reflect what they really think, merely what they think educated opinion says. So when asked to say what makes great art, they offer the "right" answers, not the ones they sincerely believe.

We hope that this test provides a stimulus to honest self-examination about what we really think about art and how important it is to us. It should encourage you to escape the confines of received or educated opinion.

Talking of received opinion, we have collected data from online players of the activity to see which factors they judge to be most important, and which of the ten artists received the highest average score.

This is the "league table" of factors that make a great work of art:

Position	Aesthetic criterion
1	The work conveys the feelings of the artist
2	The work is enjoyable
3	The work reveals an insight into reality
4	The work displays great technical ability
5	The formal features of the work are harmonious and/or beautiful
6	The work conveys an important moral lesson or helps us to live better lives

And these are the top ten artists:

1	Jane Austen
2	Shakespeare
3	Michelangelo
4	T. S. Eliot
5	Miles Davis
6	Mozart
7	Kurt Cobain
8	Pablo Picasso
9	Stephen King
10	Britney Spears

Final thoughts

It is interesting that conveying the feelings of the artist is the factor considered most important for most people when judging the greatness of art. It suggests that the romantic view of art is still the most popular one, even if it is not in the art world.

The fact that art is not expected to deliver moral or life lessons is the other striking finding. Oscar Wilde was once considered outrageous for suggesting art was beyond morality; now it seems that view is mainstream.

It's no surprise to see Britney languishing in a distant tenth place in our great artists chart, but some other results are perhaps revealing. Jane Austen comes first, even though she is often perceived to be a less substantial artist than the three heavyweight males who follow her. Maybe our rankings are fairer than those of standard opinion, with its alleged bias toward dead white males. The suggestion is even more intriguing when you consider Miles Davis's elevation above Mozart. Still, we wouldn't want to claim too much for the table, which simply reflects the opinion of Web site visitors. After all, is Kurt Cobain really better than Picasso? The suggestion smells of something, and it's not Teen Spirit.

9

Are You Officially Ethical?

When I do good, I feel good; when I do bad, I feel bad, and
that is my religion.

Abraham Lincoln

Is it possible to desire the bad? The answer may seem obvious-
ly to be yes. We desire many things that are bad for us, and others of the planet: long-haul flights, too much sweet food, sex
with inappropriate people, perhaps in inappropriate places, or
in inappropriate ways. Yet as Plato realized, there is something
odd about this. If we want something, surely it is because in
some sense at least we think it to be good. You just wouldn't
want that triple-chocolate muffin unless you thought it tasted
good, for example. And if you really, truly felt that the bad side
outweighed the good, surely you wouldn't want it anymore.

The conundrum has no easy solution. But it raises an
important issue that manifests itself in many ways: how do we
know that what we think is good is really good, or whether
what we think is bad is really bad? It is this area of moral
uncertainty that we are now entering.

Take the test

All you need to do is complete a simple questionnaire that
comes in two parts. Complete Part One before looking at Part
Two. Bear in mind the fact that we are not going to make any

judgments about what really is right or wrong. We're not trying to find out if you have the "right" moral values.

Part One

		Strongly agree	Tend to agree	Neither agree nor disagree	Tend to disagree	Strongly disagree
1	Buying organic food is in the best interests of both people and the planet.					
2	Frequent flyers who pay for CO_2 reductions to offset their emissions are taking as moral a stance on global warming as people who never fly for environmental reasons.					
3	It is always better to buy local produce than food that has been flown in from hundreds or thousands of miles away.					
4	It is not in principle wrong for powerful Western nations to use their military forces, without UN support, to overthrow tyrannical regimes.					

		Strongly agree	Tend to agree	Neither agree nor disagree	Tend to disagree	Strongly disagree
5	Every country should sign up for the Kyoto protocols, which aim to stabilize the extent of greenhouse-gas concentrations in the atmosphere.					
6	Given a choice between increasing environmental damage and cutting economic growth, it is sometimes better to increase environmental damage.					
7	Western customers should boycott companies if any of their goods are found to have been made using child labor in the developing world.					
8	Genetically modified foods have a great potential to help nourish the world.					
9	Free trade is more important than aid or certified Fair Trade for the developing world.					
10	We need to do more to resist the power of supermarkets and multinational chains.					

Part Two

OK, so you will easily see what we're doing with these questions: we're trying to find out how far your deeds match your words. But don't jump to any conclusions about how you're going to be judged—you may be surprised. Just answer honestly. As they used to tell you at school, if you don't, the only person you're cheating is yourself . . .

		True	False
1	I buy organic food whenever I possibly can.		
2	I only use a car when walking, cycling or using public transport is practically impossible.		
3	I always make sure that the food I buy has not been imported from other continents.		
4	It would be wrong to use military force, without UN support, to end a modern-day Auschwitz.		
5	My house uses all low-energy lightbulbs (fittings permitting), the household appliances I have bought all have high energy-efficiency ratings and I don't usually leave electrical appliances like TVs and video recorders on standby.		
6	In the last two years I have not taken any flights that were not strictly necessary for my work.		

		True	False
7	I have taken reasonable steps to make sure that the clothing stores I usually buy from have sound policies on the use of child, sweated and forced labor.		
8	I would rather eat non-GM foods that had been treated with four times as many pesticides than GM foods treated with a quarter of the pesticides.		
9	I always buy certified Fair Trade goods where they are available as an option, and I actively seek them out.		
10	I regularly shop in a supermarket.		

How did you score?

Your answers will generate two scores.

1 Part One measures how "officially ethical" your beliefs are. We'll come to what exactly that means soon. Here's how you get your score for Part One:

	Strongly agree	Tend to agree	Neither agree nor disagree	Tend to disagree	Strongly disagree
Qs. 1, 3, 5, 7 & 10	2	1	0	−1	−2
Qs. 2, 4, 6, 8 & 9	−2	−1	0	1	2

Total your scores, and write them in the results grid below.

2 Part Two measures how "officially ethical" your actions are. In Part Two, you simply score 2 points for every "true" answer and you lose 2 points for every false one. (Note that the questions do not match exactly the questions in Part One, but they are all about aspects of behavior covered by the values mentioned in Part One.)

Officially ethical beliefs score (Part One)	
Officially ethical actions score (Part Two)	

3 Now you can locate yourself on this graph. The horizontal axis is your score for officially ethical beliefs, and the vertical is for officially ethical actions. So, for example, if you scored +6 for officially ethical beliefs and −8 for officially ethical actions, your cross would go where our x is on the grid.

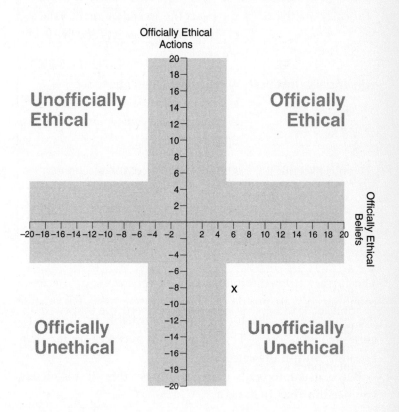

4 The section of the graph your cross is in reveals the category to which you belong. Here, in brief, is what each one means.

Officially Ethical	In both your beliefs and your actions, you exemplify the ascendant moral values of liberal Western society.
Officially Unethical	You reject the ascendant moral values of liberal Western society and live your life accordingly.
Unofficially Unethical	Although you subscribe to the ascendant moral values of liberal Western society, your actions do not live up to these ideals.
Unofficially Ethical	Although you reject the ascendant moral values of liberal Western society, you actually live your life according to them. This is very odd.

The further from the intersection of the two axes the more pronounced your profile is. Those whose crosses fall outside the gray area are absolutely, totally, certifiably in those categories, with no appeal. Those close to the gray area are also pretty solidly within the category.

But as usual, to really understand what this all this means, you need further analysis.

144

What's official about it?

On one level, this activity is a simple means of determining whether there is any significant difference between the values you espouse and those you actually live by. Of course, it would be disingenuous for us to pretend that we didn't design the questions in order to catch a good number of people out: we suspect a lot of people are "unofficially unethical."

This aspect of the test is, we think, a perfectly respectable exercise. It may well be that we can never fully live up to our ideals, but we should nonetheless be honest about how far short of them we fall. And if your cross is deep in the bottom right-hand corner—outside the gray area—then the dissonance between belief and action is pretty big.

But actually our interest goes much deeper than this. We're interested in what passes for being moral in contemporary society. Our phrase "officially ethical" has a ring of derision about it, rather like the term "politically correct" (which we don't actually like). If you look at the ethical statements put out by big business, the "ethical reports" compiled by bodies such as *Ethical Consumer* magazine, and the various columns and articles in newspapers on how to live ethically, you'll find they return again and again to a small number of core values, mainly to do with environmentalism, with asides attacking big business and free trade, with support for Fair Trade.

Between us we disagree as to which elements of this package really are ethical and which are not. (One of us is actually a pretty religious recycler and buyer of Fair Trade goods; the other throws all his rubbish straight in the bin and buys what's cheapest.) But where we agree is that we think this growing consensus is complacent and often inappropriate.

If you look again at the statements in Part One, for example,

145

you'll find that there are credible moral grounds for disagreeing with all of them. The value of organic produce is dubious. Why should frequent flyers who buy carbon offsets be considered less responsible than people who don't fly, when both contribute exactly the same to global warming? How do we balance the benefits to poor farmers in the developing world gained by importing their foodstuffs against the environmental impact of airplanes? Can't boycotting companies who have been found to use sweatshops be counterproductive? Surely we want these companies to monitor their suppliers, which means it is always possible they will uncover malpractice. If they do, it is how they respond that matters, surely. And so on. Any intelligent, thoughtful person would be able to see the case against the "officially ethical" view, even if they do not ultimately endorse it.

So actually no one should feel comfortable with their results. Each leaves you with new questions.

For the officially ethical who support and live by the new orthodoxy, your consistency of belief and action is commendable and, we suspect, rare. But maybe you should question whether the values you follow so scrupulously are the right ones.

For the unofficially unethical whose constant refrain is "I know I should be doing X and Y but . . .," maybe it is your expressed values that are wrong and not your deeds. If actions do speak louder than words, perhaps they express a better set of values.

For the officially unethical, having perhaps first thought you were going to be told off for being bad, you may now be feeling smug, as it's the official ethics of the day we are questioning. But not so fast. We are not endorsing a total rejection of all the moral values we are told we "ought" to hold, only a more critical, reflective attitude toward them. Perhaps your defiant stand is indicative of a willful contrarianism, rather than a superior moral insight.

Finally, the unofficially ethical, who recycle, buy organics and never fly yet say that these are not morally superior things to do: you're just weird.

Final thoughts

There is no reason to think the warm glow of being good is in itself a bad thing. There are some who think morality is easily debunked, if it turns out that people who do good feel good about it. The idea seems to be that ethics has to hurt, and if you actually enjoy being good you're doing it for all the wrong reasons. However, there is no reason why altruism and self-interest should usually conflict. Morality need not be a zero-sum game, in which to do good to others you have to do harm to yourself.

Nevertheless, the warm glow can become the tail wagging the dog, the purpose of "doing good" rather than just its natural accompaniment. Acting well may not always require pain and sacrifice, but knowing the right thing to do can be very difficult indeed. How much easier it is just to accept received wisdom. Ironically, many people who uncritically accept what is now "officially ethical" would actually consider themselves to be somewhat countercultural. But to replace one set of unquestioned values with another does not display much intellectual or moral rigor. If you're serious about being ethical, you're going to need to think hard and not just have a big, swelling heart.

10

Staying Alive

> If a man is alive, there is always danger that he may die, though the danger must be allowed to be less in proportion as he is dead-and-alive to begin with.
>
> Henry David Thoreau

Staying alive is something almost everyone wants to do almost all of the time. Yet do we really know what being alive means, and therefore what remaining in that state requires? The question may seem perverse, but consider how some people regard a permanent vegetative state to be a form of death, and also how some have their bodies frozen in the hope of being revived later, whereas others, who would not normally pass up a chance at a longer life, shudder at the thought.

In this activity we hope to probe your intuitions about what it takes to remain in existence. The penalty for responding incorrectly is, however, death. Whatever that means . . .

Take the challenge

The aim of the game is to stay alive. There are three rounds. In each one, you will be presented with a scenario and then offered two choices. The decisions that you make determine whether you stay alive or perish. You should always base your decisions solely on the desire to keep yourself in existence.

Take each scenario at face value—there are no "tricks"—and you do not need to worry about other "what-ifs."

At the end of the game you will discover if you have stayed alive or not, although, because this is a philosophical game, the answer won't be that straightforward . . .

Round 1: The Teletransporter Choice

You have been chosen to go on a very important mission to Mars. You have no choice in this matter; you must go. But you can choose your means of transport.

One method is teletransportation. You will step into a scanner here on Earth, which will destroy your brain and body while recording the exact states of all your cells. This information will then be transmitted to a replicator on Mars. Travelling at the speed of light, the message will take three minutes to reach its destination. The replicator will create, out of new matter, a brain and body exactly like yours. The person on Mars will look like you, think like you, in fact be indistinguishable from you. He or she will certainly feel as though they have merely fallen asleep on Earth and then woken up on Mars. This method is 100% reliable.

The other choice is to go by spaceship. This is very risky and there is a 50% chance that the ship will not complete the journey and you will die in transit. But if you do successfully take the spaceship, then your body and brain won't at any stage have been destroyed.

You must make the choice that you think will give your self the best chance of surviving.

Teletransporter or spaceship?

Round 2: The Memory Choice

Both the teletransporter and the spaceship worked without any hitches. But life on Mars turns out not to be a bed of roses. In fact, two strange viruses have evolved on the planet. The first destroys body parts. Fortunately, medical science is highly evolved and people are simply given artificial limbs and organs as required. You've been hit pretty hard by this virus and, in fact, almost your entire body is now made up of artificial parts.

However, there unfortunately exists a second virus, which attacks the brain. It is peculiarly nasty in that it doesn't destroy the brain, rather it messes up the neural pathways, leading to a loss of memory and also a change in personality traits. One person who had the virus had been a successful rock musician. Now he can't even remember what his own songs sound like, but he's become rather good at accounting. It is indeed an odd virus!

We're sad to say that you've caught the virus. Medics can get around the virus by replacing pieces of the brain with advanced forms of silicon chip. In your case, they would have to do this to almost all of your brain. But trials show that you can be sure that the result will be the total preservation of your memories, personality, plans, beliefs and so on, and a person as able to carry on living a normal life as is, well, normal.

The alternative is to succumb to the virus with its consequent loss of memory and change in character. You must make the choice that you think will give your self the biggest chance of surviving.

Take the silicon brain or let the virus do its worst?

Round 3: The Reincarnation Choice

Over time, scientists were able to repair people who made either choice. Those who chose silicon brains were given back organic ones, and those who fell victim to the virus found their personalities could stabilize.

But scientific progress also turned up an amazing discovery. Strange as it may seem, it has been discovered that reincarnation of a sort does actually occur. Apparently there is some immaterial part—call it a soul—in all human beings. On death, it leaves the body and enters the body of a newborn animal or human. It does not take memory with it, of course, for if it did we'd have known this were true already. It is thought that it may have some effect in determining one's character, but given the evidence for the strong influence of genes and upbringing, this effect is relatively small. So far, despite your strange past and odd transformations, your soul has stayed with you.

But here's the really odd thing: these souls will die if stored at below freezing point for longer than a week.

These facts are vital to the last choice you must make. You are very ill, but scientists have almost found a cure for the disease you have. Further, they have also developed a technique to "deep-freeze" humans, enabling them to be revived later with their memories and character intact. You have two choices.

The first choice is to let the disease take its toll. Your body will die, but your soul will live on—but do remember this does not preserve your memories, intentions, desires and so on. The second choice is to be deep-frozen, then thawed and cured later. This will destroy your soul and only has a 30% chance of success: that is, there is a 70% chance that the thawing and curing won't work.

You must make the choice that you think will give yourself the biggest chance of surviving.

Be frozen or let your body die?

How did you fare?

Follow your progress through this flowchart to see whether you've survived or not—and if you have, whether it is survival of mind, body or soul.

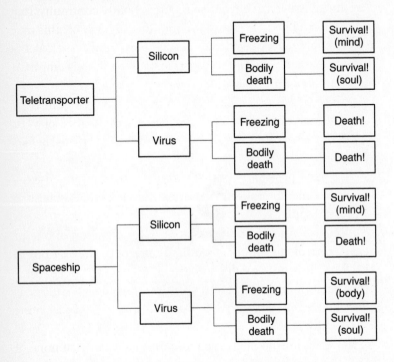

In online versions of this activity, about 60% of participants stay alive, while 40% die. But perhaps more important, what kind of survival do those who stay alive have?

What survival means

This game is based on the idea that in the history of philosophy (and indeed other branches of human thought), there are three things that have been thought of as necessary for the continued existence of your self. One is bodily continuity, that your physical body keeps on functioning. In practice, this may require only parts of the body to stay in existence, such as the brain. After all, we don't cease to exist after a limb is amputated or an organ transplanted.

The second is psychological continuity, which requires, for the continued existence of the self, the continuance of your consciousness—your thoughts, ideas, memories, plans, beliefs and so on.

The third possibility is that you need the continued existence of some kind of immaterial part of you, which might be called the soul.

It may, of course, be the case that a combination of one or more types of continuity is required for you to survive. But in this game it is not possible to keep all three forms of continuity. Therefore you are forced to choose which you think is most important for survival, even if as a matter of fact none alone really is.

However, it is possible to choose in such a way that none of these forms of continuity is maintained. In such cases, you are pronounced dead, since without continuity of body, consciousness or soul, there is nothing left of anything that is usually thought necessary to sustain the self over time. And even if you haven't died, some choices may make your survival problematic, so do continue reading, even if you are already celebrating dodging death.

First of all, two routes through the game are consistent with the theory known as psychological reductionism. According to this view, all that is required for the continued existence of the self is psychological continuity. If you are teletransported, then accept the silicon transplant and finally let your "soul" die, you preserve the continuity of consciousness required, according to this view, for you to survive. The same is true if you made the same choices, except for Round 1, in which you chose the spaceship. But if you did this, you were, in the psychological reductionist view, taking an unnecessary risk, since there was a 50/50 chance the spaceship would not have made it, taking your body, brain and consciousness with it.

However, those who reject this theory would say that you have not survived at all but fallen foul of a terrible error. In the teletransporter case, for example, was it really you that traveled to Mars or is it more correct to say that a clone or copy of you was made on Mars, while you were destroyed?

An alternative to psychological reductionism is the view that the survival of the self is essentially a matter of keeping the particular physical organism that is you alive. If you take the spaceship, let the virus change your mind and then freeze your body, killing your "soul," then you manage to stay alive in this sense.

But would this really be survival of the self? Is it enough for your body to continue to exist if your personality, wishes, beliefs, desires and memories do not? Is the self really no more than a particular animal body? Many think it is, but many others think that without some kind of psychological continuity, the self cannot survive as a body alone.

The third theory, however, is possibly the one that has historically enjoyed most popular support: you are your soul. But what does this mean? Many people probably think that, if they have a soul, that is what determines character and is the bearer of memories and so on. But this seems very implausible, given what we know about the role that the brain plays in consciousness. That's why in this game the soul is a vaguer, immaterial part.

Given the way this game is set up, as long as you finally chose to let your body die, you stay alive, in the sense of keeping your soul alive. But we have declared two routes through the game so erratic that we have decided by authorial fiat that they are tantamount to death. And no route is free from difficulties.

If your first two choices were consistent with psychological reductionism or bodily continuity, but then you went for bodily death, and with it the end of your consciousness, we give you the benefit of the doubt and allow that you were trying to keep the aspect of the self alive that you judged most likely to keep your soul with you.

But if you chose the spaceship and then allowed the virus to do its worst, and only then chose bodily death, the question arises, why did you, in the first two scenarios, choose bodily over psychological continuity? The implication seems to be that you think the soul naturally accompanies the body and so kept that alive as an appropriate "host" for the soul. But this seems to make the soul a rather empty self. It is a self that needs no continuity of thoughts, beliefs or memories to exist. It is rather a kind of immaterial home for thoughts, emotions, beliefs and so on. Is the self such a thing?

What if your first two choices before soul survival were the teletransporter and silicon? This makes the final choice very strange, since whereas the first two are clearly designed to maintain psychological continuity, in finally opting to save your soul, you ultimately dismiss mental continuity as less important. Perhaps you valued soul survival all along and simply thought that psychological continuity was the best way to achieve it, but if it came to the crunch, you'd choose the soul over your mind. This is consistent, for sure, but, to us at least, a little baffling.

You also keep your soul alive if you first chose the space-ship and then the silicon, or the teletransporter and then the virus. But for the purposes of this game we have decreed both of these as deaths. Why? Because ultimately we're testing rational consistency, and there seems to be little consistency in assuming first that the soul follows the body, then consciousness and finally neither at all; or that it follows first consciousness, then the body and then neither.

Still, one route does undoubtedly result in death. If you take the teletransporter, let the virus do its worst and then get frozen, you first destroy your original body, then your original personality and finally your original soul. Hearteningly, only 4% of people chose this, the least popular route, showing that rational inconsistency is not always the default position for humans.

Final thoughts

So what is really required for personal survival? Interestingly, when it comes to the crunch final choice, nearly two-thirds opt to keep their soul, even though it does not preserve their minds or bodies. Why is this? Perhaps because we are so used to thinking that it is our "soul" that counts, we cannot bear to allow anything that carries the name to perish. But given the way we defined *soul* for the purposes of this game, we find it surprising so many think it matters.

Of the other two views, psychological continuity is more popular than bodily continuity. In our biased opinion this is right. "I think, therefore I am" is the most famous line in philosophy, and one truth it reflects is that we are the sum of what we think, feel, believe and desire. You may disagree. But then what is this "you" that disagrees? Your body? Your soul?

11

How Free Are You?

I wish that every human life might be pure transparent freedom.

Simone de Beauvoir

Sixties rock band Cream had a big hit with a song called "I Feel Free." Judging from the lyrics and tone, this made the singer, Jack Bruce, very happy indeed. But is this joy misplaced? He may feel free, but perhaps it's no more than a feeling, and really he's not free at all. Does he even know what it would feel like *not* to be free?

Philosophical pedantry again. We know what the song means: "free" as in not constrained by others, traditional roles and values, the establishment, The Man or whatever. But there is another sense in which we all feel free almost all the time. Even if we are in chains, we can make decisions about what we would like to do and choose any physical action that restraint does not make impossible. This freedom is central to being human.

At least, most people think it is. But is this feeling of freedom a mere illusion? How free are you really?

Take the Freedom Challenge

This activity takes the form of a questionnaire. All you have to do is say for each scenario how responsible you think the person is for their actions. "Not responsible at all" means they deserve no praise or blame for their actions; "Completely responsible" means they should receive all the credit or blame for what they did. Though in English we tend to say someone is responsible only when we are blaming them, do remember that in this context it refers to due credit as well as blame.

		Not responsible at all	Partly responsible	Largely responsible	Completely responsible
1	A windsurfer not paying complete attention hits a dinghy, knocking a child overboard, who drowns.				
2	You study hard and pass your exams.				
3	A drab-looking man who has had little luck in his working life and is jealous of those who seem to have it easy doesn't defend a very successful and handsome colleague against an untrue accusation.				
4	You fall asleep at the wheel and come off the road, hitting only a tree and causing minor damage.				
5	You notice your bank has incorrectly credited your account, but you don't let them know the mistake.				

		Not responsible at all	Partly responsible	Largely responsible	Completely responsible
6	Someone from a poor, uneducated background works hard and eventually becomes a college professor.				
7	A proud colleague fails to own up to a mistake, leaving someone else to get the blame.				
8	You see a child trapped in a burning building and you rush in and save it.				
9	Driving at 35 mph in a 30-mph zone, you run over and kill a child.				
10	You give a ticket to something you really want to see to a sick stranger who has no other means of seeing it.				
11	An off-duty traffic police officer runs into a busy road to pull a child to safety.				
12	A naturally gregarious person, given to leadership, and who has worked with the disabled in the past, volunteers to take a group of disabled people on an outing.				

		Not responsible at all	Partly responsible	Largely responsible	Completely responsible
13	A mechanic hurries a safety check, leading to a brake failure but no accident.				
14	You do a good deed that you actually quite enjoy doing.				
15	A retired Second World War veteran on a state pension receives an overpayment of benefits and keeps the money.				
16	Someone donates money they had been saving for a treat to a disaster appeal.				
17	An overworked doctor who has been treating victims of a terrorist attack misprescribes a drug, leading to the death of a patient.				
18	A bystander leaps into rough seas to save a child from drowning.				
19	A sporty person volunteers to help on a sports day for children with special needs.				

		Not responsible at all	Partly responsible	Largely responsible	Completely responsible
20	One of your character weaknesses leads you to make a decision that gets someone else in trouble.				
21	An ATM gives someone too much money and they don't try to return it.				
22	A child wins the school prize for effort.				
23	A single mother donates what for her is a large sum of money to a charity for the relief of famine after seeing a television program about starvation.				
24	A volunteer classroom assistant lets some children out of his sight in a national park with grizzly bears roaming. The children are found safe.				

How to score

Once again, the scoring here may look complicated, but follow the instructions step by step and all will be revealed.

1 Fill in the grid opposite, giving a score determined by the answer you gave for each question. So, for example, if you answered "Partly responsible" for question 9, write in "1" in the blank space next to 9 (row *a*, column A):

o = Not responsible at all

1 = Partly responsible

2 = Largely responsible

3 = Completely responsible

	Question no.	A		Question no.	B		Question no.	C	
a	9			1			17		
b	4			13			24		
c	5			21			15		
d	20			7			3		
		D			E			F	J
e	2			22			6		
f	8			18			11		
g	10			16			23		
h	14			19			12		
		G			H			I	K
					Grand total				

You now need to do some adding up, which will give us a variety of data to help interpret the results. There are two sets of four numbers in each of columns A, B and C: those for rows *a–d* and those for rows *e–h*. (For example, your scores for questions 9, 4, 5 and 20 are the first set of four in column A; your scores for questions 2, 8, 10 and 14, the second set of four in column A.)

2 Add up each set of four numbers in columns A, B and C, entering them into boxes D, E, F, G, H and I.

3 Then, in J write the sum of D + E + F, and in K write the sum of G + H + I.

4 Add up J and K and enter it in the "Grand total" box.

The really interesting part of the analysis is yet to come, but first, the overall verdict: what your grand total score means.

72 You think we all have absolute free will at all times.

60–71 You ascribe to human beings a very high degree of free will over their actions.

45–59 You are more than willing to accept that human beings do not always act entirely freely.

30–44 You do not think human beings act completely of their own free will much of the time.

1–29 You think all this talk of free will is largely nonsense.

0 You're an out-and-out determinist.

Now let's see what it all really means . . .

How free do you really think we are?

The questions asked you to say how responsible various people, including you yourself, would be in a variety of circumstances. The idea of responsibility is very closely tied to that of freedom: on many accounts, someone can only be responsible for what they do if they could have done otherwise. Therefore, our ideas about responsibility—whether we think we are responsible for our actions or not—give us a good idea about whether we think we act freely or not.

The overall score you have already calculated gives you a general indication of how much you ascribe responsibility to individuals for their actions. This result probably won't surprise you: you'll already know if you tend to excuse people or hold them to account.

But the other scores enable you to see if there are any variations within this general world view. To help make this clearer, it is useful to write the scores for D–K into the last column on the grid on the next page.

D	You are the agent and the outcomes are bad	
E	An undescribed other is the agent and the outcomes are bad	
F	A partially described other is the agent and the outcomes are bad	
G	You are the agent and the outcomes are good	
H	An undescribed other is the agent and the outcomes are good	
I	A partially described other is the agent and the outcomes are good	
J	Total for actions with bad consequences	
K	Total for actions with good consequences	

First, we can see what difference it makes whom you are thinking of. Compare the figures in D, E and F. They should be the same, since the scenarios we presented you with came in comparable—though not identical—sets of three, and each one of D, E and F corresponds to one of these sets. But, in fact, though the scenarios were comparable, the people in them were not. You were the agent in the scenarios for D; in E it was a more or less anonymous other; and F corresponds to a third party whom we gave you more information about, factors that may affect your judgment. Did you judge all three equally, or did you hold some more responsible than others (resulting in a higher score)?

The same three scenario types apply to G, H and I. So these, too, should be the same. But there is one other difference that needs to be factored in. If you look at the subtotals D to I, then D, E and F are the responsibility scores for actions with bad outcomes; G, H and I those for actions with good or neutral outcomes. In general, we tend to blame others more for acts with bad consequences than we do ourselves (and also, generally speaking, ascribe more responsibility to individuals for actions that have bad outcomes, rather than neutral outcomes, regardless of the intent behind the action). Social psychologists call this kind of inconsistent reasoning a *fundamental attribution error*. If you have made this error, then E will be higher than D. In addition, the more we know about mitigating circumstances, the more we tend to forgive, so F will often be lower than E. One interesting question: did you judge yourself more harshly than others whose mitigating circumstances you knew about?

Similarly, we tend to give ourselves more credit for actions that turn out well than we do others. This is called the *self-serving attributional bias*. So we would generally expect G to be higher than H, which in turn will be higher than I, because when we see people's specific motives for doing good things, we tend to think they are less worthy of praise for them. "They would do that, wouldn't they?" we say.

If you compare J and K you can determine if in general you tend to think people are more responsible for their actions when what they do has bad consequences rather than good, or vice versa.

That's not the end of the interesting comparisons, though. Read across every row in the main results grid, and you'll see if you judged individual comparable actions differently. These are the types of action that each scenario was an example of, with the letter for the rows that contain your responsibility rating for them:

a.   Negligence leading to death

b.   Negligence leading to minor damage

c.   Opportunity taken to cheat

d.   Act of meanness resulting from character flaw

e.   Hard work leading to success

f.   Opportunity taken to be heroic

g.   Tough choice taken to be selfless

h.   Good act resulting from a character trait

There are endless comparisons you can make here, and we hope you find it interesting to explore them. Take, for instance, the scores on row *a*, for negligence leading to death. Many people are quick to condemn others who act in this way, but they more readily forgive themselves. Did you judge all three agents the same?

Or compare these scores with the ones for row *b*, negligence leading to minor damage. As in row *a*, people made mistakes that could have been fatal. It was mere chance that in one case death resulted and in the other it did not. If chance was the only difference, then, rationally speaking, people should be just as responsible in both rows.

In general, then, if you have a clear and consistent outlook on the scope of human freedom and responsibility, there should be negligible differences between comparable sets of scores: D to I should be within a couple of points of each other, as should J and K. If, however, there are significant variations, then we suggest you are not consistent in your view of human freedom. The most pessimistic interpretation of this is that you ascribe freedom to people when it suits you to do so and not when it doesn't: for example, you are happy to take credit for your successes but not blame for your failures. That may be natural. But do you think it's right?

Final thoughts

Human free will is for many a cornerstone of their beliefs about human nature, dignity and morality. Doubt we are free and, so it is said, you doubt our very humanity. Nothing in this activity helps settle the question of whether that is true, or whether we do indeed have free will. Rather, we are trying to question whether belief in free will is indispensable after all.

Our suggestion is that commonsense beliefs held by millions of people already allow for the fact that we are not always entirely responsible for the choices we make. Hardly anyone therefore seems to think that human beings without absolute free will are unimaginable. So, our final thought here is, would it really be so terrible if our belief in the reality of free will were eroded a little further? How much can we give up the idea of freedom? More perhaps than is usually allowed. Of course, you are, or seem to be, free to disagree.

12

The Ultimate Philosophy Quiz

Now, what I want is, Facts . . . Facts alone are wanted in life.

Charles Dickens, *Hard Times*

It is often said that philosophy is more about know-how than know-that. Facts have their place, but it is more important to be able to think clearly.

We agree. But factual recall can be very useful. It is easier to learn from the great philosophers of the past if you can actually remember what they said. And let's not forget that being able to reel off dates and names can be very impressive in social situations, making you look much more clever than you are. Clear thinking can leave slower minds baffled; erudition leaves them dazzled.

So we conclude our book with a good old-fashioned philosophical quiz. And if you don't know most of the answers, just think—you will by the end. Fingers on the buzzers . . .

Round 1: Places

1 Where was Bertrand Russell imprisoned during the First World War?

a. Holloway   b. Reading

c. Brixton   d. Pentonville

2 Where did Kant live and work his whole life?
    a. Leipzig   b. Königsberg
    c. Heidelberg   d. Berlin

3 Whose youth was Socrates condemned to death for corrupting?
    a. Athens   b. Rome
    c. Alexandria   d. Carthage

4 In which Paris cemetery are Jean-Paul Sartre and Simone de Beauvoir buried?
    a. Montparnasse   b. Montmartre
    c. Rive Gauche   d. Sacré-Cœur

5 From which Dutch city's Jewish community was Spinoza excommunicated?
    a. The Hague   b. Leiden
    c. Haarlem   d. Amsterdam

6 Where did Descartes die?
    a. Anjou   b. Paris
    c. Stockholm   d. Brussels

7 In which London cemetery is Marx buried?
    a. Hampstead   b. Battersea
    c. Golders Green   d. Highgate

8 Which of the following was NOT born in France?
    a. Albert Camus   b. Jean-Paul Sartre
    c. Simone de Beauvoir   d. Auguste Comte

9 What part of the brain is the seat of the soul, according to Descartes?

   a. The hippocampus   b. The pineal gland

   c. The corpus callosum   d. The hypothalamus

10 Where is Buridan's Ass?

   a. In Buridan   b. In the Platonic world of forms

   c. Between two haystacks   d. On twin-earth

Round 2: Quotations

Who said . . .

11 "Woman is not yet capable of friendship: women are still cats and birds."

   a. Spinoza   b. Plato

   c. Aristotle   d. Nietzsche

12 "What we cannot speak about we must pass over in silence."

   a. Aristotle   b. Sartre

   c. Kripke   d. Wittgenstein

13 "Vertigo is anguish to the extent that I am afraid not of falling over the precipice, but of throwing myself over."

   a. Kierkegaard   b. Schopenhauer

   c. Sartre   d. Nietzsche

14 "The condition of man . . . is a condition of war of everyone against everyone."

   a. Locke   b. Marx

   c. Nietzsche   d. Hobbes

15 "'Tis not contrary to reason to prefer the destruction of the whole world to the scratching of my finger."
    a. Hume   b. Nietzsche
    c. Wittgenstein   d. Hobbes

16 "Religion is the sigh of the oppressed creature, the heart of a heartless world, and the soul of soulless conditions."
    a. Kierkegaard   b. Marx
    c. Schopenhauer   d. Nietzsche

17 "Life must be lived forward, but can only be understood backward."
    a. Kierkegaard   b. Nietzsche
    c. Wittgenstein   d. Sartre

18 "It is better to be Socrates dissatisfied than a pig satisfied."
    a. Locke   b. Hume
    c. Mill   d. Hobbes

19 "Give me chastity and continence, but not yet."
    a. Seneca   b. Augustine
    c. Spinoza   d. Anselm

20 "Death is nothing to us, since when we are, death has not come, and when death has come, we are not."
    a. Epicurus   b. Democritus
    c. Seneca   d. Socrates

Round 3: Dates

21 In which year was Socrates condemned to death? (see question 3)

a. 399 BC   b. 299 BC

c. 199 BC   d. 99 BC

22 In which year did John Locke die?

a. 1550   b. 1704

c. 1750   d. 1850

23 Spinoza's *Ethics* was published the same year as his death. Which year was that?

a. 1577   b. 1677

c. 1777   d. 1877

24 In which century did David Hume live and work?

a. 16th   b. 17th

c. 18th   d. 19th

25 Kant's *Critique of Pure Reason* was published in which year?

a. 1581   b. 1681

c. 1781   d. 1881

26 In which year did Bertrand Russell publish his first great book, *The Principles of Mathematics*?

a. 1903   b. 1908

c. 1913   d. 1918

27 In which year was John Stuart Mill's *On Liberty* published?

a. 1709   b. 1759

c. 1809   d. 1859

28 In which year did Michel Foucault die?

    a. 1884   b. 1948

    c. 1984   d. 1994

29 In which year was the publication of Marx's *Capital* completed?

    a. 1833   b. 1853

    c. 1873   d. 1893

30 In which year did Nietzsche die?

    a. 1880   b. 1900

    c. 1920   d. 1940

Round 4: Works

31 Who wrote *An Introduction to the Principles of Morals and Legislation* in 1789?

    a. John Stuart Mill   b. Thomas Hobbes

    c. Thomas Reid   d. Jeremy Bentham

32 Who wrote *Language, Truth and Logic*?

    a. A. J. Ayer   b. Ludwig Wittgenstein

    c. J. L. Austin   d. Gilbert Ryle

33 Which was the only of Wittgenstein's works to be published in his lifetime?

    a. *Tractatus Logico-Philosophicus*

    b. *Philosophical Investigations*

    c. *On Certainty*

    d. *Remarks on the Foundations of Mathematics*

34 Who is the author of *Anarchy, State and Utopia*?
   a. John Rawls
   b. Robert Nozick
   c. Mikhail Bakunin
   d. Thomas Moore

35 With whom did Bertrand Russell write *Principia Mathematica*?
   a. G. E. Moore
   b. Frank Ramsey
   c. Ludwig Wittgenstein
   d. Alfred North Whitehead

36 Who wrote *The Consolation of Philosophy*?
   a. Alain de Botton
   b. Boethius
   c. Lucretius
   d. Seneca

37 Which of the following is NOT a book by Kierkegaard?
   a. *Repetition*
   b. *Either/Or*
   c. *Fear and Loathing*
   d. *The Sickness Unto Death*

38 Who wrote *The Varieties of Religious Experience*?
   a. William James
   b. Thomas Aquinas
   c. St. Anselm
   d. Søren Kierkegaard

39 Who wrote *The Open Society and Its Enemies*?
   a. Isaiah Berlin
   b. Bertrand Russell
   c. Karl Popper
   d. Antony Flew

40 In which book did Nietzsche address the question of why he wrote such good books?
   a. *Thus Spake Zarathustra*
   b. *Ecce Homo*
   c. *The Anti-Christ*
   d. *The Gay Science*

Round 5: Theories and Principles

41 Which principle is associated with the Vienna circle?
   a. The principle of double effect
   b. The Carnap-Schlick principle
   c. The verification principle
   d. Heisenberg's uncertainty principle

42 Which principle demands that we do not multiply entities beyond necessity?
   a. Occam's razor   b. Hume's fork
   c. Moore's minimizer   d. Plato's dialectic

43 What is the name of the fallacy of conflating two different meanings of a word?
   a. Equivocation   b. Bifurcation
   c. Semantic assent   d. Type/token confusion

44 Who created the idea of a category mistake?
   a. Bertrand Russell   b. Aristotle
   c. A. J. Ayer   d. Gilbert Ryle

45 Which of these is not a philosophical principle or argument?
   a. Hume's fork   b. Pascal's wager
   c. Foucault's pendulum   d. Occam's razor

46 Who developed the metaphysical system known as the monadology?
   a. Spinoza   b. Leibniz
   c. Husserl   d. Erasmus

47 Which political ideology is associated with the philosophy of Edmund Burke?
a. Liberalism   b. Conservatism
c. Libertarianism   d. Socialism

48 Which political ideology is linked with the philosophy of Mikhail Bakunin?
a. Anarchism   b. Liberalism
c. Conservatism   d. Socialism

49 Which philosophical school is most closely associated with Dewey and Peirce?
a. Emotivism   b. Pragmatism
c. Logical positivism   d. Idealism

50 What was Paul Feyerabend against, according to the title of his best-known book?
a. Theory   b. Reason
c. Morality   d. Method

Round 6: Miscellaneous

51 What is the name of the argument that tries to show that God is a being who necessarily exists?
a. Teleological argument   b. Ontological argument
c. Cosmological argument   d. Deontological argument

52 What distinguishes an *ad hominem* argument?
a. It is associated with a particular individual
b. It attacks the person rather than their arguments
c. It appeals to universal human nature
d. It is decisive

53 Which country did neither Locke, Berkeley nor Hume come from?

    a. England   b. Ireland

    c. Scotland   d. Wales

54 According to the etymology of the word, a *philosopher* is a lover of what?

    a. Truth   b. Science

    c. Life   d. Wisdom

55 What did eighteenth-century Enlightenment philosopher Rousseau confess about his children?

    a. He beat them

    b. He gave them all up to orphanages

    c. He refused to let them mix with other children

    d. He couldn't have any

56 In which position did Albert Camus play soccer?

    a. Goalkeeper   b. Defense

    c. Midfield   d. Attack

57 Which of the following declined the Nobel Prize for Literature?

    a. Albert Camus   b. Bertrand Russell

    c. Jean-Paul Sartre   d. Martin Heidegger

58 What did Wittgenstein allegedly threaten Popper with in 1946?

    a. An axe   b. Public humiliation

    c. A poker   d. His fists

59 Which philosopher killed his wife?

    a. Louis Althusser   b. Paul Feyerabend

    c. Herbert Marcuse   d. Friedrich Nietzsche

60 Who attempted to refute Berkeley's idealism by kicking a stone?

a. James Boswell   b. David Hume

c. Samuel Pepys   d. Samuel Johnson

How did you score?

Here are the answers:

1	c	11	d	21	a	31	d	41	c	51	b
2	b	12	d	22	b	32	a	42	a	52	b
3	a	13	c	23	b	33	a	43	a	53	d
4	a	14	d	24	c	34	b	44	d	54	d
5	d	15	a	25	c	35	d	45	c	55	b
6	c	16	b	26	a	36	b	46	b	56	a
7	d	17	a	27	d	37	c	47	b	57	c
8	a	18	c	28	c	38	a	48	a	58	c
9	b	19	b	29	d	39	c	49	b	59	a
10	c	20	a	30	b	40	b	50	d	60	d

No deep analysis this time, just our opinionated, judgmental assessment of what your scores mean.

50+   What you don't know about philosophy isn't worth knowing.

36–49   What you know about philosophy is well worth knowing.

23–35   What you know about philosophy is just worth knowing.

11–22   What you don't know about philosophy is worth knowing.

<10   What you know about philosophy isn't worth knowing.

JULIAN BAGGINI

> "This book is like the **Sudoku of moral philosophy**: apply your mind to any of its 'thought experiments' while stuck on the subway and quickly be transported out of rush-hour hell."
> —*New Statesman*

Plume
A member of Penguin Group (USA) Inc.
www.penguin.com